Choosing
A Path

Choosing
A Path

Sri Swami Rama

Published by

**HIMALAYAN INTERNATIONAL INSTITUTE
OF YOGA SCIENCE & PHILOSOPHY
OF THE U.S.A.**

Honesdale, Pennsylvania

© 1982, © 1996 by The Himalayan International Institute
of Yoga Science and Philosophy of the U.S.A.
RR 1, Box 400
Honesdale, Pennsylvania 18431-9706 U.S.A.

Fourth Printing 1998

Library of Congress Catalog Card Number: 81-85538
ISBN 0-89389-077-4

Contents

Acknowledgments

We thank dear Dr. Arpita and dear Barbara Bova for going through the transcriptions and typing the manuscript. We also thank Kevin Hoffman, Dale Colton, Dr. Susan Thornburg, and Charles Blanchard for their enthusiasm in getting this book together. Patrice Hafford typeset this book with great endurance and completed it in a matter of a few days. Mr. Randy Padorr-Black designed the book cover.

Foreword

This book is derived from transcriptions of the tapes of Swamiji's lectures delivered during seminars at the Himalayan Institute. We decided to bring these lectures into the form of a book. We are publishing this book for the benefit of those who want to choose a path for self-improvement and unfoldment. I am sure that seekers will be inspired by these lectures.

This book is a practical guide that describes all the major paths of enlightenment. Though various are the paths, the goal is only one. Every human being has a unique quality, and every seeker is gifted with something extraordinary. Everyone is unique in his or her own way. After realization of that extraordinary quality, one can tread the path and not waste his or her time and energy window-shopping in the market of spirituality.

This book is organized into seven main chapters. The first one prepares the student for choosing a path, and the remaining ones describe the major paths of yoga: jnana, bhakti, karma, raja, laya, and the various methods of kundalini awakening, including tantra. After becoming aware of one's natural tendencies and talents, one can select and practice the path that is best suited to his or her inclinations and situation.

Swamiji's clear and profound descriptions of these paths will inspire and guide sincere students in their efforts for attainment. The information and understanding provided in Swamiji's descriptions of the paths of yoga come from his own direct experience, for he was trained from childhood in all the yogic disciplines, and his burning desire to understand the reality and know the truth motivated him to personally examine and experience all the methods reported. Having traversed the entire terrain, he can provide a broad perspective and a detailed knowledge that helps the student see his or her way more clearly and avoid pitfalls and detours. Such a wealth of information is extremely rare; that it is being shared so openly is a great gift of love.

May all aspirants be open to receiving, understanding, and utilizing these precious teachings, and may they be inspired to learn more and work eagerly for their self-enlightenment.

In eternal gratitude and service,

ARPITA, PH. D.

Preface

Why?

All the great religions of the world fundamentally are one and the same. They serve the different groups in certain ways to some extent, but do not satisfy the intellectuals. Therefore, it becomes important for everyone to have freedom from religious dogmas so that all may search for truth and understand the various paths followed by the great men in the past. In choosing a path, three considerations seem to be important: time, training, and desire.

Time here means that if the seeker at a proper time starts practicing and following a particular path, he can surely complete the voyage in this lifetime. When the mind is clouded and congested by the suggestions found in books, the seeker rarely gets an opportunity to study his own abilities. A time comes when he desires to attain something higher, but he doesn't find himself capable because he has become too old. The body does not function according to his desire, the mind slips to the old grooves of past habits, and practice remains a haunting dream for him.

Religions teach us to have faith in God but the mind cannot stop questioning. Even though one has faith in God, the mysteries of life still remain veiled and the prime questions of life remain unanswered. All the philosophies and religions have one and the same aim, and that is to know thyself. But the training that is imparted in our childhood does not seem to have any such educational program that really helps us in Self-realization. Comforts we obtain, pleasures we experience, but the questions still remain unanswered.

The question, "Do the existing religions serve the purpose of modern man or do they create more obstacles for him?" should carefully be examined. I am not against any religion as such, but if there is no freedom of thinking, it is not possible for individuals to understand the way of life nor to attain its purpose. Therefore the first requisite is mental freedom, and that is possible only when one has the opportunity to contemplate on the prime questions of life: Who am I? From where have I come? What is the purpose of my existence here? Where will I go from here? The religious bibles of the world have their conclusions based solely on faith. But blind faith is more dangerous than being an atheist. Having faith in God is wonderful, but the way it is explained to us is shallow and does not satisfy the curiosity of the learned aspirants. Suppose one does not believe in God, and yet there are those who believe. What difference does it make in either case? Intellectual curiosity is not at all satisfied with believing or not believing. The existing bibles of the world finally instruct their followers to study the book of life—the very Self—on all levels: external environment, body, senses, breath, conscious mind, unconscious mind, and that which exists behind all these levels of life. Modern science says that a human being is made out of certain material components and that there is no proof of any self-existent reality or God as described by religionists. But there is another group of researchers who have researched the interior life in its totality and have come out with a definite conclusion that ultimate Truth—the center of cosmic Consciousness—exists eternally, and that when one turns within he can experience peace, happiness, and bliss. He can know himself and come out with the answers for the questions he has been brooding upon. He ultimately finds that his self is the Self of all and his individuality is a superimposition created by his ignorance. When he crosses the mire of delusion created by his mind, he obtains freedom. He is free from all pains, fears, and miseries.

The religionists out of fear believe in God; the modern scientists out of ignorance do not believe in the existence of the ultimate Reality; the atheists out of disgust do not want to search for the Truth because they see that religionists have been exploiting human beings in the name of God for ages. But atheists have no philosophy to support their belief. Agnosticism and atheism are alike in a certain respect. I am with them as far as not being influenced by formulas, dogmas, and doctrines. But I take one step ahead and say that interior research should be continued. Scientists and atheists have no proof that the ultimate Reality does not exist. And religionists cannot prove that it does because they lead their followers through that faith which remains unexamined.

There is a vast difference between religion and spirituality. A religion is a set of dogmas, doctrines, and rituals. A student of religion is not allowed to think or search beyond these sets of rules. But in spirituality, all the human resources are directed toward the search for the spirit only—the ultimate Truth. In religion, faith is never challenged, but in the path of spirituality, faith is established with the help of reasoning based upon direct experience. A spiritual human being can be religious, but a religious human being is not necessarily spiritual. This book does not offer religious rules, dogmas, or rituals but leads the seeker to choose a path for himself by examining his potentials and abilities. As all jackets do not fit one person, so is the case with religious beliefs. Religious beliefs are engrained in the tender and innocent soil of human hearts and minds. These may create serious barriers in the search for and the exploration of Truth. Real spirituality dawns through self effort, sincerity, and inner wisdom.

When, with the help of direct experience, we examine the sayings of the great sages and closely study their lives, we find that they have touched that peak of enlightenment. As a result they became totally selfless, serving others and loving others without any self interest. These great men, though having trodden different paths, attained one and the same goal which is freedom, happiness, and bliss.

Some of these paths will be explained in this book in order to inspire seekers to choose for themselves. The desire for seeking should not die. When the seeking dies a human being still remains alive, but such a state of complacency is injurious for his growth and ultimately for humanity. In such a case prolonging the span of life becomes worthless. The search for truth alone provides a ray of hope for the individual and for humanity as a whole. Do we not realize that this generation of ours is in a state of stagnation and that we are not attaining the next step of civilization? We have done so much research on matter, mind, and energy, yet we have not discovered the ways and methods of attaining happiness and loving others selflessly. Though we all know that the life span here is brief, yet we do not make efforts and apply all our resources to know life and its purpose. This book gives a glimpse and creates a provocative atmosphere for the intelligent and learned so that they will begin studying their inclination to follow a particular path, and so that they don't waste time and energy in the prevailing confusion of our times, but choose a definite path for themselves.

As an observer and student of philosophy and religions, I would like to mention that the trends of Western religions today are more toward intellectualization, and little effort is being made in the interior research of spiritual life. For lack of spiritual practicality in their religious and cultural training, when Western students try to follow the inner paths, they suffer and waste time in experimenting on one path and then another rather than following one path consistently. Western students, though having immense emotional, methodical, and intellectual abilities, suffer because of their limited cultural and educational background, which is externally oriented. This does not provide them with the opportunity to search independently within the interior levels of their beings.

Another factor which is noticeable is that Western students shun discipline. All modern students lack patience. They want to have results quickly without making sincere efforts. These cultural weaknesses are deep-rooted in the habits of Western students. In Western culture, no one is allowed to think freely about the spiritual dimensions of life. They are rigid in their religious beliefs, though they are free to think the way they want in leading their external lives. Those who want to seek the path of inner life are made to think that they are heathens, that they cannot be saved, and that they will go to hell. The guilt and fear created by such doctrines cripple the talents of western aspirants. They are forced to believe that anything outside their religion is not authentic.

Westerners often compare the technological advancements of the East and West and conclude that because the East is not technologically advanced, the spirituality of the East is worthless and invalid. This prejudice does not allow Western students to study the spiritual paths sincerely. The younger generation today is longing to seek something new and afresh, but it is torn by the conflicts created by guilt and fear. With these views in mind and to serve the needs of aspirants and free-thinkers, I present this book.

That is why.

Chapter
1

Preparation for Choosing a Path

In order to understand and choose a path for enlightenment, one should thoroughly understand the philosophical and psychological foundations on which the various paths are based, for without this basic knowledge it is not possible to understand the different paths in their proper perspective. Before one is actually ready to choose a path for himself, he must understand the internal and external architecture of life, and then alone determine to practice the philosophy that he has chosen. Philosophy is not mere speculation related only to the thinking world, nor is it merely an expression of societal or religious norms. One's philosophy should be built, just like a mansion, and then one should live in it. There are countless books on philosophy, but they do not satisfy the seeker's inner quest, for they do not offer concrete methods of practice.

In building a practical philosophy of life, one should first learn to understand the nature of the external world, the world that is subject to sense perception, the world of matter, forms, and names; that which occupies the human mind and dissipates its energy. External knowledge—the knowledge of the objects of the world—though essential, is a gross aspect of knowledge, therefore is only partial knowledge, and partial knowledge is like a half truth, which is not truth at all. When we start questioning life and its problems, we become introspective and realize that the mind is clouded and cannot see clearly enough to make subtle discriminations and proper decisions at the proper time. The external world does not supply correct data, for everything is swiftly moving and constantly changing. We want to experience and know the ultimate reality, but everything moves rapidly, changing its form and thus its qualities. The mind, too, is influenced by its habit of identifying with the objects of the world, so it is not capable of recording things as they are. In such a case, there is no clarity of mind, and if the mind is not one-pointed, it is dissipated. Such a disordered, uncontrolled, and untrained mind is not able to understand the ultimate reality.

The objects of the world have their importance. They have some meaning, but they are not fully satisfying because of their constantly changing patterns; they are subject to decay, destruction, and death. Something gratifies the senses today, and so we become happy momentarily, thinking that we are attaining something great. But after some time, that particular thing changes—its quality and form change, and again we are disappointed. Human beings live in a world that goes to decay, yet they become very attached to the continually changing objects of the world. So they always remain insecure and scared. Some people are obsessed by food, some by sleep, some by sex, and some by self-preservation. One finds out that somehow or other he is always obsessed by something and that he is never free from that obsession. But even so-called enjoyments are so marred by fears that fear becomes predominant and controls life.

People are afraid to examine their fears, but one should learn to examine his fears properly to find out how valid they are. Most fears are based on imagination and are rarely examined. One does not have to go back to the past to know his fears; they can easily be analyzed. One should learn to watch his fears carefully, to avoid becoming their victim and to avoid strengthening them by brooding on them. It is not of much use living in the world with fears. How can one enjoy anything if he lives with fear? One thinks that he might lose what he has, or that he won't obtain what he wants to have. Fear actually leads him to pain and misery.

It is important for the aspirant to structure the world around him in such a way that it does not create barriers to self-unfoldment. The external world becomes an obstacle and constantly distracts the mind. It is not possible to live without the objects of the external world, but they have their limitations. Modern man's concept is that it is very difficult to be spiritual and at the same time conduct one's duties, but this is not true. It is one's inner attitude that makes all the difference. When Maharshi Ramana was asked for his definition of sin, he said, "Sin is that which affects the inner mind." If the mind is not affected by a particular thought or action, then it is not a sin. But if one's mind becomes a victim of negativity and passivity and creates a guilt feeling, then it is a sin. If one is not strong within, if one is easily swayed, then he can never be happy. One needs to be strong and coordinated from within first before he performs his actions and speech accurately. Inner strength is very important.

Citizen of Two Worlds

In trying to understand the nature of the world and in forming a solid philosophy of life, we must realize that we are the citizens of two worlds: the world within and the world outside. A great disagreement exists between these two worlds; we want something and the outside world obstructs us from obtaining it. There is a particular desire, but our society or our family does not permit us to fulfill that desire. There is often a conflict and competition between our desires and the interests of our families and society. Most of us create external crutches for the sake of security, but, alas, the external objects of the world, no matter how many we own, are not capable of making us happy. This fact has been examined by the sages since time immemorial. Even so, human society continues to follow the path of materialism without understanding the importance of spirituality. Superficial beliefs of religion and mere promises of the scriptures do not fulfill the needs of modern society.

No individual wants to act the way society wants him to, but one cannot live in society without having consideration for others. In such confusing circumstances as are created by the man-made moral codes, one could isolate himself and devote his time and energy to worshiping his ego and finally become totally egotistical and uncommunicative. But human beings have the capacity and ability to go beyond these confusions by being truthful to themselves. We should live in society, but we should realize two facts about daily life. First, we should not create obstacles for ourselves, and second, we should not disturb others. If our actions are conducted with these two considerations, then we will have the time and ability to do interior research.

We can learn to organize our thoughts and actions in such a way that our desires do not create obstacles for ourselves or others. When one learns to analyze his desires, he comes to understand which desires are helpful for him. Desires can be chosen by understanding how they arise and function and what their consequences are. The faculty of discrimination helps us to judge which desires yield results that are helpful, and which do not. Those desires that create obstacles should be shunned completely, but the desires that are helpful should always be strengthened. Such helpful desires should be brought into action. Control of unhealthy desires is not repression or suppression. Control means that we have realized that a desire is not healthy and that we are gathering together all our energies and directing those energies toward one healthy goal. But in repression and suppression we suffer because of stress and we are still victims of those desires.

Most people remain strangers to themselves, and yet they want to be friends with others, and they claim to love others. But if one does not know himself, how can he know or love others? Therefore, it becomes necessary to understand the nature of the self, the nature of the people with whom one lives, and the nature of the universe. By understanding these, one might be disappointed in some ways, but he will know the Reality. Very few people are conscious of the many dimensions of life within. That is why they have many inner conflicts—which they project outside onto others, so that life outside also becomes gloomy.

The Physical Body—Garment of the Self

What do we mean by *self?* When we talk about self, we should clearly understand which part of self we are talking about. We only introduce a mere part of ourselves to the world. The first part of our whole self that we strongly remain aware of is the body. The body is a very important instrument for us; it is an essential garment that we are wearing. We are not the body, although we each have a body. Nevertheless, we identify with the body. For example, we say, "*I* have a headache." In our modern day-to-day language, we do not accept that we are not the body. But if a human being is the body, then why do we immediately dispose of a dead lifeless body? Because we know that the body is separate from the life force.

According to Eastern philosophy, the body is a compound of five elements, called *tattvas:* earth, water, fire, air, and space. If there is an imbalance in any of these five elements, then we become ill. We are like jars filled with these elements; when the jar is broken, water goes to water, fire goes to fire, air goes to air—each goes to its respective element. Most people do not even really know much about themselves physically. They do not realize how wonderfully their body is constructed. Those who know something about anatomy tell us that if the lungs were removed and spread out, they would cover several miles. We have over ten billion brain cells, and every cell has a world of its own in it. A human being is like a galaxy, having ten billion worlds within it that work together beautifully. Another amazing thing is that a cut heals by itself even without any treatment because the blood cells rush to the damaged part to help it, to cure it. There is perfect understanding in our internal organization that works for the well-being of the city of life. There are subtle principles that govern our body structure and its coordination on many levels. These subtle principles exist on higher levels and govern the body. When we come in touch with those principles we can heal ourselves in any eventuality. Even a serious disease can be cured by spiritual and mental forces provided we know how to voluntarily utilize and direct the energy from the energy centers and principles that govern the body. How can this coordination exist without our awareness? It is because there is a deeper and more subtle system within that governs both the body and mind.

Besides the five elements, the physical body also consists of the five cognitive senses: smelling, hearing, touching, tasting, and seeing. And we have five active senses also: with our feet we walk, with our hands we work, with our mouth we chew our food and talk, and, finally, we have the organs of elimination to cleanse the body. So our bodies are actually a compound made of the five elements, the five cognitive senses, and the five gross senses. The physical body depends on food, which contains pranic energy, though in a gross form. But the body cannot be sustained by food and its energy alone. A more subtle form of pranic energy is supplied to our bodies through breathing.

The physical body is not our only property. There are many dimensions within us, and we should know them all equally in a systematic way. There are two caretakers of this body, called inhalation and exhalation. They continually guard the city of life without any interruption; they always do their duties faithfully. One is always busy in cleansing, and the other is busy in nourishing. Anyone who is conscious of health should understand these two mechanisms. Even if one is supplying a nutritious diet to his body, he can still create toxins, and if he does not eliminate them properly, he will always be unhealthy. Bad breathing habits can disturb the digestive system by disrupting inhalation and exhalation and other pranic vehicles. Negative thoughts convert the nutrients of food into poison. Thus the body builds up toxins. Inhalation and exhalation are like two caretakers whose duties are regulated by our mental life. By studying their behavior and regulating them, we can prevent them from creating many physical disorders. That which guides and directs these caretakers should also be understood.

Mind—the Greatest Friend and Foe

We are not only bodies, we are not only breathing beings, we are also thinking beings. Our thinking process is more complex than the mechanism of our bodies and the functioning of our pranic vehicles. Qualitatively, thought is stronger than the physical and pranic strength. The strength of consciouness is much higher than the strength of thoughts and pranas. There are many modifications of our minds that deal with different necessities of life both within and without. The mind functions in the internal world, as well as the external world. It all depends on how the mind is trained and which part of life receives more attention.

Every person thinks in a different way, and the individual

ego seems to govern life. If someone tells us, "This is the truth, why do you not accept it?" the ego does not want to accept it, although we know it is the truth. There are very few people in the world who are prepared to hear the truth, even though many people claim to speak the truth. The liquor of the senses is very intoxicating, and people constantly drink the charms and temptations of the world, which blinds their vision. People never think that they can be wrong. Even if they are punished, they are not prepared to accept the idea of being wrong. Discrimination is a great quality of the mind, provided it is allowed to develop properly. The mind is our greatest friend, and it wants to help us. It does not want to create problems for us, but it is in the habit of going according to the way we train it. If we want to steal something, the mind says, "It doesn't matter, nobody is looking. It's not wrong." The mind will tell us this because the mind is a great helper. This is the job of the mind, to help us whenever we want and however we want. If someone wants to become a murderer, the mind will help him, and if he wants to become a sage, the mind will also help him. So there is nothing wrong with the mind. The mind is our greatest friend and foe both, but we have to train it not to create obstacles for us. Mind is not a problem creator; rather, lack of training is the very basis of disharmony. Proper training of the mind is the essence of all successes.

There are various faculties of mind, and all the faculties need to be cultivated with a sense for fulfilling the purpose of life. Ego seems to be the strongest one, and it must be trained, purified, and prepared to fathom the deeper level of our being. Such a higher ego can help make the mind focus inward. Most human beings have a lower ego that closes the doors to learning, and that is why they suffer. They suffer, not because they do not want to understand things, but   because they are ignorant. Ignorance means lack of knowledge, just as darkness means lack of light. Neither has any existence of its own. People are very close to the Reality, yet they are not aware of it because their individual thinking prevents them from knowing it. It is like being asleep. In sleep we are not aware of our existence, though we exist. If two people go to see a sage but one of them sleeps and the other remains awake and converses with the sage, then, although both are very close to the sage, only the one who is awake experiences his presence. Every human being is close to the Reality, but they are not aware of it. Only the awakened ones have direct knowledge of it. The scriptures tell us, "Wake up from the sleep of ignorance, and do not slip back to sleep!" That darkness of ignorance is the lack of knowledge of the Reality.

Meeting That Which Functions Within

What is this knowledge that human beings are not aware of? There are two kinds of knowledge: the knowledge that helps one in knowing the external world, and the knowledge that helps one in knowing oneself. After one understands the body, he must then set about to understand how the physical body is linked with the inner body. The inner body, that which functions inside, is called *antahkarana;* the physical body moves because of the functioning of antahkarana. Who is that inner being? We all know that when we think and understand, we do not realize the source of knowledge. What is that power behind and beyond our thinking that really provokes and motivates the mind to think, to understand, to analyze, to decide? What is that power that moves us, that keeps us alive? Everyone understands the thinking process in certain degrees and grades, but only a fortunate few understand beyond the spheres of mind. A difficulty arises at this point because one needs to prepare oneself to understand that which is beyond. Our instruments are so gross that they can analyze only external things, and they cannot make us aware of why these things are changing. When we use our minds to analyze, we find that the mind itself is also subject to change, that it is changing every second. So it is also important to study and understand the mind.

When one starts studying life, he first starts examining it practically and learns about his body, relationships, and the objects of the world. A careful examination of the various levels of the external world—growth of the body, stability of relationships, and changing patterns of the objects of the world—makes him feel that the external world cannot offer all the solutions of life. Then he starts turning within, in search of peace of mind, happiness, bliss, and freedom. Typically, he will try to find someone he can trust as a guide, a teacher, a messiah. So he starts studying the sayings of the great sages. Then he begins to understand something more about life. Every human being wants something to believe in. But there has been no teacher or prophet ever born on the earth who said, "My children, don't make any efforts. I will do everything for you. Just take my hand and you will be liberated." No guide has ever said this. All the great teachers have formulated a system of discipline to be followed by their students. All the great teachers have said, "You are capable of enlightening yourself! I can show you the path, but I cannot push you to the state of enlightenment." A great murderer and bandit named Valmiki, who later became the author of the *Ramayana,* met a sage who transformed his life by making him aware of the Truth. Valmiki was enlightened and became a great sage and poet. So is the case of the great poet Kalidasa. He was an idiot, rejected by his wife, who later became famous and is today considered the Shakespeare of the East. In every human life a moment comes when one finds an opportunity to improve and unfold oneself, provided that moment is not engulfed with inertia and sloth. Human history is full of such examples. We can have that ability if we rightly choose to follow the path of spirituality. Therefore, disappointment has no place in life. We always have the opportunity, the place, time, and means to attain the purpose of life.

In the cycle of evolution a human being has attained a status and intelligence that enables him to survey the whole of life. He has all the potentials and means to grow and develop himself, but not everyone utilizes these means. By following a definite path, the aspirant can attain the purpose of life. Inability in choosing a path, or not practicing the discipline of the chosen path, wastes one's time and energy. Various are the paths, but the goal is only one. Life on this platform is our own choice, and it is also our choice whether or not to follow the inner path and get enlightened in this lifetime.

We choose our own people and environment. Our birth is also our choice. It is our choice the way we want to live. We create relationships in the world and become attached to our creations, with the thought that the relationships and objects of the world are the objects of love and will help us grow. But we do not learn to love unless our consciousness is expanded to its fullest capacity.

When a dear friend or relative dies, we become a sage and philosopher for a few moments. We think, "This person was with us yesterday and he was so nice. Now look what has happened to him. The same thing could happen to us. Life on this earth is an illusion." Suddenly everyone turns into a pseudo-sage. But when we go back to our homes, everything returns to the way it was before. Even though nature and reality give us the opportunity to realize the Truth, we still remain blind because of our strong attachments.

The Method for Inner Study

Human beings are always disappointed in the external world, yet they have not turned inward to understand anything about the internal world. Those who begin to search the other dimensions of life come in contact with subtleties that are puzzling to them, and they do not know what to do next. People have been trained from childhood to observe, examine, and verify the things in the external world, but no one has taught them how to look within, how to verify within, and how to know within. The ancients contemplated on these issues for a long time, and they developed a method for studying the inner world. Just as modern scientists developed a method for analyzing the nature of matter, so there is a positive and exact system that tells us how to analyze and understand inner life.

Many people ask, for example, "Is there anything like a soul within us?" Modern philosophers deny any such entity because they are influenced by materialistic science. But are we really sure what science is? A few years ago, a Midwestern university sent out thousands of letters asking various scientists for their definition of science. The responses did not establish any clear-cut definition of science, so even the meaning of science is not defined as yet. According to ancient yogis, however, science means *vijnanam,* the systematized and organized study that leads one to attain all the states of *jnana*— knowledge. Science is a way of knowing through the intellect; science is an external expression of inner knowledge.

If anyone wants to be a student of the interior world, of the path of light, if he wants to do inner research, he will have to understand this point: one must have a purified, free, and one-pointed mind to know and examine the interior Self. If the mind is not free, if one is prejudiced from the very beginning, influenced by a particular set of dogmas, doctrines, or formulas, then one can neither conduct nor complete any research. For conducting research within, one should be truthful, sincere, and free from prejudices. Research should not be shaded by social and cultural norms or religious fanaticism. It requires a totally independent and unbiased mind. One cannot lie to oneself. One should ask, "Am I really true to myself? Am I really a seeker?"

In doing research within, we have to completely forget our prejudices from the past, and we have to remain true to ourselves; otherwise our research will be incomplete. Second, we must start training the mind to be inward. But the mind does not want to be inward; it wants to focus outside, because it has been trained and educated to know the external world only. The mind does not want to go toward the more subtle world within; it does not understand the concept of thinking without an object. We can imagine things, but imagination depends on an image within. We must train the mind to go inside to our personal world, which is responsible for all our actions and speech in the external world, so that we can understand those needs, motivations, desires, those strong powers within us that move us to do something in the external world. We want to know their nature. We want to know why we act and feel the way we do.

We let the external world affect us more than it should. Many people remain very unhappy because others have suggested that they are not good people, and they have accepted these negative suggestions from others. Those suggestions have become a part of their lives, so they think of themselves as bad people. But when someone condemns himself, excludes himself, creates guilt feelings within himself, or when he thinks that he is good for nothing, he is committing a serious mistake. On the other hand, we also create miseries for ourselves when we remain indifferent to the external world and when, because of our habits, we do whatever we want without understanding the consequences.

If we are in the habit of creating miseries for ourselves, can we really blame God or anyone else? The ancient philosophy of the sages says, "O human being, you have the capacity to understand yourself, to understand both *klista* and *aklista*— that which is helpful for you, and that which creates obstacles for you." Most of the miseries we suffer are çreated by ourselves, but we put the blame on others. Our miseries are not created by Providence, by the sun, moon, and stars, by our environment, nor by people—and never by God. We ourselves have created our miseries, and if we want to understand this truthfully, we will have to turn the mind inward.

The mind must be trained to go inward and examine itself because it is not accustomed to practicing a technique of inwardness. Just as one needs a specialist to find out what disease he has, one has to be a specialist in understanding himself because the mind is in the habit of playing tricks. The method of knowing mental life is called psychology. It is very easy to find out something about a person by watching his actions—how he moves, how he talks, how he looks at others, how he smiles, how he cries, how he eats, how he sits, and how he makes certain gestures. One can discover a great deal about the inner life by studying body language. So when we start turning within, we do not have to ignore the external world, nor do we have to make any radical change in our external life. Which language we speak and which garments we wear are not of much value as far as Self-realization is concerned. People waste much time and energy in getting attached to brands and labels and forming a sect or cult. Thus the whole purpose is lost, and one is caught by the diversity of rituals and the fanaticism of cultism. We simply have to be ourselves and create a strong desire to know ourselves from within. That desire is the first requirement. If one doesn't understand the importance of spirituality and meditation, then he should not waste his time and energy with it. If one is not convinced that meditation is a technique that is helpful, if one is not prepared, then he should not apply that technique. Because if he does, there will be no result; there will only be disappointment. So first, to research the inner world, one needs a burning desire to know his inner potentials and states.

When we look within, we realize that the mind has two

parts. The part that we already know is called the conscious part, and that which is unknown to us is called the unconscious part. The subconscious is a part of the unconscious. It means that which is submerged, that which is not visible. If the conscious part of mind does not function, the creative and dynamic aspect of human life will be crippled. And if it is destroyed, then there will be no coordination between body and mind. When this occurs, death is the result. But even after this separation, the unconscious mind remains intact. Let us now examine the unconscious mind. When we look at something, the sensation that we receive is carried through the optic nerve to the brain and then to the conscious mind. Then it settles down in the unconscious mind as a sensation that leaves an imprint there. Looking at something with interest will help us to remember it if we ever see it again. But if we look at something casually and don't pay much attention to it, then even though we are seeing it, we are not registering it. Registration happens because the mind has much interest in seeing something, and memory depends on interest. There is no camera that registers as fast as the brain. The fastest speed is not the speed of light, but the speed of mind. People can think so fast that no computer can register their thinking. And when we think, everything we are registering is stored in the unconscious mind.

The Four Main States of Consciousness

The unconscious is also a vehicle for the center of consciousness, from where consciousness flows on all levels. Ordinarily, people remain in body consciousness only; they are conscious of the body, of their relationships, of what they have, and of the objects they do not have. But look at what happens to that level of consciousness when one goes to deep sleep. The wife for whom one lives, the child for whom one would die, the property for which one would fight—one suddenly loses awareness of them. One goes to that state of unconsciousness and totally forgets everything. So we are not only the citizens of two worlds, the external and the internal; we are also the inner dwellers of three states—waking, dreaming, and sleeping. We are awake for many hours, we dream, and then we go to deep sleep. Every individual has his own private world, and this is called the world of dreams and sleep. We also create worlds around us and outside us during our waking state with our relationships, roles, belongings, and possessions.

Even though one has examined all three of these states, still he remains unchanged and untransformed. A fool goes to sleep, and he wakes up as a fool. His personality is not transformed overnight; there is no change. Then what makes a sage? One becomes a sage if he attains the fourth state, called *turiya,* the state beyond.

The best part of human civilization and culture is not found in any particular era, culture, or country. It is that ageless universal wisdom which has been given by those great people who attained this fourth state. They give new hope to humanity and to those who really want to attain the higher level of consciousness. In the first three states—waking, dreaming, and sleeping—one thinks that he is full of sins, pains, problems, and weaknesses. But the great ones say that if he were to attain the fourth state, he would be free from these self-created complexes. And it is possible for everyone to attain that state. It is just like being in a mansion with four stories. If one is on the ground floor, he can see the landscape, but his vision is limited. The horizon that he sees is entirely different from the one he would see if he went to the second floor. And if he went to the third floor, it would look different again. But when one goes to the fourth floor, the whole horizon is quite clear, and he is able to see far and wide. Every human being is fully equipped to attain that state. Then why is everyone not attaining it? Because one does not remain constantly aware of the reality, and one is distracted by the objects of the world. Thus the short but precious span of life is wasted in vain by dwelling in the external world. There are some people who become aware of this fact, but they are not capable of bringing their thinking into action. "The thought which is not brought into action is either treachery or abortion."

To bring right thought into action means to establish a bridge between the internal and external ways of life. The weak are lost in the external world, but the strong make sincere efforts to create the bridge between inner and external life. This is the way of living a conflict-free life. Unless one finds out whether he is action oriented, selfless-service motivated, intellectually inclined, or desires to be in silence, he or she will remain unfulfilled. These qualities are the symptoms that help one to choose a path.

Often, the conscience within whispers silently and warns the human being that the mortal world is not a fully satisfying world, and that there is something beyond it. The objects of the external world disappoint everyone, and a stage comes when one starts searching other dimensions of life. It is possible for one to live peacefully in the busiest and most crowded cities of the world provided he learns to practice a systematic way of understanding his own internal states. The world around us is very small and can be measured, but the world within us is vast and unmeasurable. To study the inner world one has to learn to sit still and to regulate the breathing system so that the pranic vehicles are not disturbed. Then he will be able to discover something about his internal states.

Becoming an Inner Dweller

To rightly conduct one's duties in the world, one should learn to be an insider so that one gains strength to cope with the stress and strain of the world. As we regulate our habits for food and sleep, so we should also learn to sit still and relax, to breathe, and make our minds one-pointed. This way, we give rest to our muscles and nervous system, and we regulate our pranic vehicles by establishing harmony in our breathing. When we talk about mind and its one-pointedness, we should not forget that silencing the mind helps to still the body and harmonize the breath. The method of meditation is not related to the mind only. One has to understand one's own body and regulate the breath behavior before one tries to practice meditation. Practicing meditation is one of the necessities in modern life, and it is especially helpful for mental health, without which physical health has less importance. When we start working with our mind, the body and breath create distractions, and the mind gets agitated. The more one wants to silence the mind, the more stressed it becomes. That's why students do not experience the joy of meditation and contemplation. The joy that one experiences during meditation is a peculiar joy and inexplicable, unlike the other joys of the world. A fortunate few experience silence. In the external world it is good for the mind to become active. But in meditation, one is in search of something that cannot be found outside. Those who do not understand the method of meditation think that meditation makes one passive. Actually, the art of meditating helps one to establish orderly control over the mind so that one can become active, and yet remain relaxed and unaffected by external stimuli. The mind is our only instrument for measuring objects in the external world, but we will have to make the mind orderly so that we can know if there is anything beyond it. And there is.

Deciding on a Path

Everyone is seeking something higher. Everyone wants to accomplish something so that he can be fulfilled completely, but completion is not found anywhere in the external world. Finally one tries to look within, and ordinarily such a seeker does not find any definite path to know, study, and attain inner peace and happiness. If the seeking does not die and the desire for seeking continues, then he starts studying the sayings of the great sages and spiritual leaders such as Krishna, Buddha, Moses, and Christ. He studies the lives and works of these great men, which inspires him, and the search is intensified. This is the crossroads for such an aspirant, when he gets the opportunity and finds the necessity of following a definite path of enlightenment. If his search persists with full sincerity and devotion, a time comes when he starts realizing that the path of enlightenment is the highest of all. When one becomes aware of the Reality and knows the nature of the transitory world, he wants to find and choose a path for himself. There are various paths to choose from, and all the paths are equally valid. Practicing faithfully only one path leads the student beyond the delusion created by the transitory nature of the world. At first the student acquires knowledge of *apara vidya*—the knowledge of the known: of the waking, dreaming, and sleeping states, of the five cognitive senses, the five gross senses, and the five elements of the body. Then he determines to attain *para vidya*—knowledge beyond. Until this point, one is doing intellectual gymnastics, because he is accustomed to living in the world of objects. But now he wants to go to the world beyond objects, and the mind is unable to conceptualize it. If the body is still and the breath calm, the mind can be calmed as well, and then one can let that which has been beneath, that which is beyond, come forward.

Enjoying the Objects of the World

Everyone should give that opportunity to himself, but many are afraid to. People are not satisfied with the world as it is, but they are accustomed to living in the world of the known, and they are afraid of the unknown. They are not sure of the path, they are not sure of their means, and they are not sure of their capacity. Here in the world, people are insecure; even when they prepare themselves, they are not sure. And insecurity is one of the causes of misery.

Many people become afraid when they start meditating and contemplating on the unknown. They complain that they might lose consciousness. This arises when the mind wants to cross the boundary beyond the world of objects. People are not accustomed to doing that, and so they become afraid. All those who really have meditated for some time struggle at this point. They have to go through this. But after one has crossed that point, then there comes a period that is free from indecisiveness. The final hurdle is when one crosses the boundary and goes beyond the world of objects into the world that has no objects.

There are people who are always dissatisfied, and there are some people who know how to be satisfied no matter what they have. There are others who are dissatisfied with the known and are afraid of the unknown. Yet there are many whose consciousness never awakens. They remain victims of *tamas* and of attachment toward the objects of sense gratifications. Those who know how to enjoy life without objects are called students of life. When one has convinced himself to be a student of life, with a strong desire to know the mysteries of life, then a point comes when he realizes that the Self, this real Self, is the Self of all. He opens his eyes. When he meets another he thinks, "Oh! This is me! Though you have a body different from my body, you are me also. I don't like to hurt myself, so how can I hurt others? Why would I want to hurt myself?" When one encounters this truth, then his consciousness starts expanding. Then he can never hurt, harm, or injure anyone; he will never consciously do that.

People should learn to appreciate and admire themselves and to have more self-confidence, so they can succeed. People constantly identify themselves with that which they are not, with the objects of the world. They forget their true Self, separating themselves from the whole, and turning themselves from the absolute truth. They will have to understand more about themselves, about their relationships with other beings and the cosmos. Finally, they will accept that they are part and parcel of the cosmos. Essentially, one cannot separate oneself from the cosmos. We are born out of it, we are in it, we return to it, and we are there all the time. We are an inseparable part of eternity. We will have to realize that.

When one develops a strong desire to know oneself, he will discover that there are happy corners in life within. Yet he has been caught by a whirlpool of sadness by becoming attached to the things of the external world. Such people do not realize that life is really very brief, just like a bubble. A bubble rises, it bursts, and then it subsides into the ocean again. An individual life is exactly like that. Everyone should learn that it is possible to enjoy life. Many ignorant people think that in trying to know themselves, they will be ignoring their duty, but they are not really engaged in the process of knowing themselves. People do not have to isolate themselves or live in an abnormal way to really know themselves. They just have to be that which they already are. That's all.

Realization of Truth alone emancipates one. "Everything of the world should be used skillfully, but God alone should be loved." It is possible for every human being to be aware of the Truth all the time and discharge his duties skillfully.

Learning to Know Oneself

The first requirement in this process is that if one does not create problems or obstacles for oneself or for others, then he will not have any conflict outside. Then he will have enough time, and his mind will have enough ability to study his inner life. Those who are seekers do not create conflict for themselves or others. They have a strong desire to search within and know themselves. Some seekers want to know themselves on all spheres. First they want to know directly how their body moves, why they are making certain gestures. This means that the internal states are the cause of these movements. One cannot know the mind without knowing the link between the body and mind, which is called *prana,* the vital force, and when one becomes aware of his internal states he finds that it is more important to know the mind. The first sheath one learns about is the physical sheath, the body made out of food. Then the second sheath is the pranic sheath, that finer body inside it which is made out of energy. Then comes the thinking process, the mental sheath. People want to know the mind immediately without knowing the pranic body, but this is not possible. The pranic body creates obstacles, and one cannot know the mind until he understands it.

Before one chooses or follows any path, he will have to have the basic knowledge about body, pranic vehicles, mind and its various functions—and he will have to have a strong desire for knowing the Truth. What is Truth? Truth is that which is not subject to change, that which was never born and will never die, that which does not need any support from any other quarter, that which is self-existent, eternal, and never changes in the past, present, or future. So we are in search of Truth, and we are applying all our means, anything that we have, to know Truth. We are trying to accomplish something in life, to find Truth. We have examined the nature of the external world and its objects but we did not find Truth. So now we are trying to go inside, to find out if we can discover that Truth which is beyond time, space, and causation, that which is self-existent and eternal, that which fulfills human life.

If I live and I am not comfortable with myself, it means there is something wrong and I should know the reason. So first of all I have to know myself on all dimensions, and then I will find out that I have the capacity to know that absolute Truth which is the prime goal of human life. Many people think that this might take several lifetimes, and many others think it can be done instantly. But the timing depends upon the power of one's desire to attain Truth. One can do it in five minutes' time, one can do it in one lifetime, or one can never do it.

When one is committed to himself, when he wants to know himself, then he chooses a path. One doesn't choose a path first and them commit. First one has to have commitment toward the purpose of life. This means he will have to take responsibility for knowing himself. He will have to learn to choose his path by understanding his own inclinations, thinking process, emotions, and actions. By understanding more about one's life, environment, mind, action, and speech, one can find out how sincere he is. One will have to learn to judge himself, to determine how far he would like to tread the path, and to know if he is sincere enough to do it or not. People know if they are sincerely treading the path or not. One cannot follow if he is not ready. If one is not ready, he cannot follow anything. So first one should prepare oneself and only then should one choose the way.

The Paths of Yoga

What is the way? Various are the ways: the path of action, *karma yoga;* the path of love, *bhakti yoga;* the path of knowledge, *jnana yoga;* the path of *raja yoga;* the path of *laya yoga;* and the path of *kundalini yoga,* which deals with awakening the dormant power within. Included in the discussion of kundalini yoga are *hatha yoga, pranayama, nada yoga, mantra yoga,* and *Sri Vidya.* All the paths lead to that same height from which one can see here, there, and everywhere. Then everything is clear. A person might disagree with someone's path, but he can never disagree with the goal, for the goal is one and the same.

Karma means action, and all actions produce certain

fruits. Those fruits again inspire us to do more actions, and consequently many other fruits are reaped. One action leads us to another action, and this creates a whirlpool around us, which we don't know how to come out of. What is involved in karma or action? The doer is involved in it. Without the wish and consent of the doer, how can one act? It's not possible. If I don't have any intention to act, any thought that I will do it, then no work will be performed by me. So every action is initially a thought. What is a thought? How do we think? We are thinking with the help of images. There are innumerable images in our minds. We are relating one image to another, and this creates a thought pattern that prompts us to do actions. But emotion is deeper and stronger than our ordinary thinking process. One single emotion can disturb the entire thinking process. Emotional power can also be useful, provided it is directed to the center of Consciousness. Many sages have used this power to attain the highest state of ecstasy—union with Divinity. In fact, the power of emotion is one of the greatest powers. Emotion is beyond all the faculties of mind. It resides down deep in a source that is not in the domain of the thinking process; it is beyond the field of thinking. Emotions have their roots in desires. So if one learns to control and direct his desires, he becomes victorious. The battle will favorably be over. Mahatma Gandhi used to say that if a person can reduce his individual desire to the level of zero, he will be free. And Aurobindo said that if someone directs all his desires toward self-enlightenment, to awakening the latent power within, then it will arise, and grace, the descending power of the Lord, will dawn. When one awakens that dormant human potential within, called kundalini, then he reaches the highest state.

The path of karma yoga is the path in which one does his actions and offers the fruits of those actions to others. Then he is free, he is liberated, he is not caught in the whirlpool of the fruits of his actions. In the path of knowledge, one uses the mind to discriminate the real from the unreal until he realizes the Truth and is one with that. The path of love makes proper use of emotions. The word *emotion* is often used in a negative way, but emotion is also a great positive power, and many great people in the world have used it to attain a state of ecstasy. This is the quickest way. Raja yoga is a path that is very systematized and scientific. In the path of kundalini yoga, one understands that there is a great reservoir within, a power within, which lies dormant. By awakening that dormant force within, one can reach the final goal.

Regardless of the path one chooses, the first step in self-transformation is to feel, "I will, I can, and I have to." So one should learn to face the reality. It will be scary, but it is necessary. And one should also gain strength and not try to escape from life. It never helps. One should face life, and for facing life one needs strength; for strength one needs self-confidence and self-discipline. But one should work systematically and gradually within one's capacity. To abruptly and blindly start to follow the path, any path, is just to regress to childhood and accept retardation. All the teachings lead to independence, and if one has attained an independent mind so that he can choose his internal path, then he is doing justice to his personal thinking process. So before one chooses a path, he should build his own personal status in his own inner world. He must have a philosophy. No matter which path he chooses, no matter which religion, which cultural background he comes from, this is something that he has to develop for his own unfoldment. There is nothing like a knowledge that is so vast, or a God that is so far away that one can never attain it in this lifetime. All of us have individual responsibility toward ourselves, and we are fully equipped. We all have the means and opportunities we need to attain a state of freedom.

Everyone has individuality, with certain special qualities, and by knowing them one can have inner courage for treading the paths of light and liberation. The purpose of these paths is to help people in expanding their individual consciousness. The gist of my experience and the experience of the other sages with whom I have lived is that we have to enlighten ourselves. One day I told my master, "If you are enlightened, then why do you not give me enlightenment too? It's too much for me. You tell me to do this, you tell me to do that—and I have been doing it, and still I don't find any remarkable change in my personality." All students think in this same foolish way; it is natural. My master said, "I am going to set you right. I am going to show you that this is not my mistake, but your mistake." I asked, "Where am I committing a mistake?" Then he told one of the swamis to blindfold me, and he gave me a bowl with a hole in it. He told me to hold the bowl. Then he started pouring milk in it, but all the milk that he poured in, drained out. He said, "Am I giving you milk?" I said, "Yes." "Why are you not retaining it?" Then he took off the blindfold, and I found that there was a hole in the bowl. He said, "There is also a hole in your head; whatever I give, it drains. You will have to patch that hole."

If someone thinks a teacher will pat his head and give him nectar and enlighten him, he is wrong. No one does that. Christ touched many students, so why were people still ignorant during that time? Moses had great powers. Why did people remain ignorant during that time? During the time of Buddha, why were people still suffering and ignorant? It was not the mistake of Christ, Moses, or Buddha. Krishna was enlightened. Then why could he not stop the battle between the Kuravas and the Pandavas? Great people lead those who are prepared. If they are not prepared, then they cannot help. Each person has to light his own lamp. If a student has oil, wick, and the lamp, the teacher will light it. But if he doesn't have these, what shall the teacher light? The teacher can guide the student, but the student should learn to accept a program for himself, for his unfoldment, for his health, for his growth. That is called a self-training program. If the student finds any obstacles, then the teacher helps him. He also makes the student aware of where he is committing mistakes. But self-improvement depends on one's sincerity, capacity, and ability.

The gist of all my advice is that one should learn to discipline oneself. Discipline means guiding one's energy properly in three directions: mind, action, and speech. Discipline does not mean arresting oneself, repressing oneself, suppressing oneself, or torturing oneself. It means learning to guide the energies that one has and learning to be positive in life. Negativity does not help. It is like slow poison. But positive thinking is like nectar, and it definitely helps.

It is important for all seekers and aspirants to choose a definite path and practice it. Without practice nothing can be attained. Blessed are those who are on the path. One day they will reach their goal and attain freedom from all pains and miseries.

Chapter 2

Jnana Yoga
The Path of Knowledge and Intellect

Jnana yoga is the path of wisdom through intellect—*buddhi.* This philosophy is the highest and most profound philosophy of the world. The word *philosophy* is not understood properly and is defined incorrectly by many people who do not treat the subject carefully. Philosophy does not mean thinking in any way one wishes or is inclined to think. Everyone seems to be a "philosopher," but few people have a solid philosophy behind them. The word *philosophy* is comprised of two Greek words, "philos" (love) and "sophia" (knowledge). It literally means "love for knowledge." Philosophy is not love of factual knowledge; it is love of the knowledge of life, knowledge of the ultimate Reality.

Every human being is pulled by love for something—love for self, for some object, or for someone to whom he is attached. But this love for objects is petty. Love for people who fulfill one's needs and whose needs one fulfills is also petty. Why do people say they love one another? Why can they not live without each other? Because they feel incomplete and insecure, and they want to be fulfilled. The ignorant expect others to fulfill this desire. If one does not take time from his petty loves, how can he develop a taste for the love of knowledge?

When one is finally fed up with all the little loves, he awakens and realizes there is something more than the love of momentary pleasures with all their limitations. No matter how great the little joys seem, there is limitation in these joys that come from loving the objects of the world. People want their joys to last forever, but these pleasures are momentary and cannot last, because all the things of the world change; they go to death, decay, and destruction. So people continually replace them. Love that is dependent on some object is not love at all. Eventually, one begins to understand the disappointment and chaos inherent in love dependent on objects, on what is external. Then one starts wondering logically about life and its value, about his relationship with the universe, and his relationship with the absolute Reality behind it. He wants to know the height of perfection which is beyond all knowing. Many people are searching, but they are bathing in the waters of materialism. They are looking in the wrong direction, so they never find peace.

The finest of all loves is the love that has no object—the love of knowledge. The highest of all desires is the desire to know the ultimate Reality, to know that Truth that fulfills us. Searching and seeking die without practice, and without searching and seeking, attainment is not possible. Practice means making sincere efforts, with all one's actions, speech, and mind, to know that highest of all loves called the love for knowledge and for truth. This is the highest of quests, and it does not involve love for any object. If one learns to live by accepting all the objects of joy and pleasure in the world as a means in his quest, there will be no problem in understanding the philosophy of life.

Love should find its way upward. Love of the truth is the highest love of all. Is there any way to learn how to love without any object? Have we learned to love the life force itself, or do we love life because we have a body? After one examines all aspects of life and realizes that he is not only a physical being, but that he is also a thinking being who can understand what is right and what is wrong, and who can sometimes control the mind, then he wants to study the other dimensions of life, and he turns his mind inward. This requires withdrawing from the senses and their objects for some time because the senses dissipate the mind and lead it outward toward the objects of the world. There are two methods to turn within: by training the senses, and by training the mind. Jnana yoga says that knowing the mind is the way, and it shows how to know, control, and direct the mind.

The philosophy of Vedanta is studied by those on the path of jnana yoga. This philosophy deals directly with the highest of all human desires—the desire to know the Truth—and it gives an explanation of what Truth means and shows the practical way of realizing it. Truth is that which is not subject to change, death, decay, and destruction. It never changes at any time, it was never born, and will never die. It is self-existent and does not depend on anything. Jnana yoga is the science that provides a systematized and organized method of study in order to fulfill this desire to know the Truth.

Life is like a manuscript, and each individual person is an author of that manuscript. In this manuscript of life, some of the pages are missing—the beginning and end have been misplaced, and one cannot recollect what he has written in them. He has only the middle portion with him, and that portion tells what he is in this present life. He knows he is here, but he does not know from where he has come, why he has come, or where he will go.

These are the vital questions in life, but no book in the world can answer them. No matter how many scriptures and sayings and books of all the great religions and philosophies of the world one studies, these questions will still remain un-answered. People always find out about life in general through indirect means—through the thinking, the writing, and the teaching of others. But this kind of information does not provide real knowledge of life. One can brood on philosophical propositions for many years, and this kind of intellectual probing can be very pleasant and helpful, but one will still not be satisfied. The mind will continue to pose questions, and as long as the mind poses questions, peace is not possible. One knows from within that the study of scriptures alone cannot satisfy one's real curiosity. Books are made up of mere dark words. How can light come from such darkness? Books can help one understand and communicate with others about certain facts in the world, but they cannot give direct knowledge of life or realization of oneself and beyond.

Only by studying the present portion of one's own manuscript, of one's own life, is it possible to know life. To know oneself directly, one has to understand life both from within and without. To know this, one has to know the *antahkarana*, "the one who functions within." The way to start in learning to know oneself is by studying that portion of the manuscript that is already in one's possession—the present, the now. By studying this middle portion of the manuscript, one can also make a link with the lost pages.

Know Thyself

First one has to know the answer to the question, "Who am I?" To do that he has to use his intellect. In this path, intellect is sharpened and purified to discriminate, decide, and judge. When an individual sharpens and purifies the intellect, when he guides it to the inner world, then such an intellect acquires the ability called superintelligence (*prajna*). With the help of this ability, one can start fathoming the deeper levels of his being and can study his antahkarana, his internal states. If one does not know and understand his inner functionings, he is not ready to follow the path of wisdom, no matter if he has studied many scriptures or earned many degrees. To know this inner being, one has to learn the ways of the sages and how they practiced the Truth.

The aim of life is Self-realization. The saying, "Know thyself," was written on the temple of the oracle at Delphi in ancient Greece. This is where East and West meet. Both Eastern and Western philosophies agree on this goal, but they hold two different ways for attaining it. East and West are actually two philosophical concepts. The Western concept goes from the gross to the grosser to the grossest aspects of life. It says that by knowing the universe, the whole external world, one will eventually know oneself. This is the belief of Aristotle. He believed in being practical, in treating the whole self for health and happiness. His teacher, Plato, held the opposite view; he believed in treating a person directly by going within to the source of the problem. There seems to be a deep influence of Upanishadic philosophy on Plato's concept of life. His whole philosophy is influenced by the philosophy of the Upanishads. This is the Eastern concept, which is based on the study of "Who am I?" Eastern philosophy moves inward from the gross to the subtle and then to the subtlemost center of Reality within. This view says that without knowing oneself on all dimensions, knowing the world or others is of no use.

The philosophy of Vedanta also says that searching for oneself by going outside does not help. It explains that if one really wants to understand the world and the universe, he should understand himself on all levels first. This system explains how to begin this process by learning about one's own body and behavior, which are expressions of the antahkarana, and then how to learn other finer states of life. The method of Vedanta leads one systematically inward and focuses on the different functions of antahkarana within. The mind is a wall between the seeker and the truth. If one's mind is not purified, one-pointed, organized, and orderly, then he cannot have a taste for this higher knowledge, and he will never attain knowledge of the Truth. When the mind is purified, then it does not create obstructions for attaining higher knowledge. Therefore, jnana yoga shows how to purify, sharpen, and train the intellect so it will be a useful instrument in the quest for Truth.

This path of wisdom is very difficult for common people to follow. It is said to be sharp—as sharp as the edge of a razor. This path is dangerous because the intellect can make mistakes, it can mislead the seeker. If someone gets on the wrong train, if he misses one turn, he will go toward the wrong direction and miss his destination entirely. For treading this path, the aspirant has to know the method of contemplation thoroughly. The first step in this path is to know the antahkarana—the internal functions—and the second step is to purify it. If the instrument is faulty or if one misuses it, he will be collecting incorrect data, and he will never reach his destination.

So to know the Truth, one first has to learn to purify his intellect. Jnana yoga is the path of Vedanta philosophy in which *atma bodha*—knowledge of the Self—is the way of realization. Knowledge of the Self means knowledge of the whole being in its totality and entirety. There are two sides of our being. One is the mortal aspect and the other is the immortal aspect. First the intellect is trained to discriminate between these two aspects of life, then it is trained to contemplate on the immortal aspect of life. It is the knowledge of immortality that really gives fulfillment and freedom from all bonds, miseries, and illusions. Actually, in Vedanta, such a discriminative faculty is called *buddhi,* and not the mere intellect as commonly understood. Jnana yoga and the philosophy of Vedanta teach the student how to train the intellect— buddhi. The word *Vedanta* means "the finer part of the Vedas," which are the storehouse of knowledge, the most ancient scriptures in the library of man today. The word *veda* means "to know," and the finest part of the Vedas is Vedanta, where knowledge ends and beyond which there is nothing to be known. The goal of Vedanta philosophy is not *samadhi,* as that of raja yoga, but to attain a state of *samahitam,* in which all questions are resolved and one attains the highest state of wisdom.

This is a voyage from intellect to enlightenment, but before anyone can go on this voyage, he has to perfect and understand himself on all levels. If one wants to have the highest love of all, he has to know himself on all dimensions. And if anyone really wants to know all dimensions of himself, the most important part to be known is the antahkarana, the inner functionings. If someone doesn't know his soul—Atman—it does not matter because it exists anyway. The individual soul does not exist because of the individual—it exists on its own. An individual's existence is because of the existence of his individual soul; one's believing or not believing, depending or not depending, having faith or not having faith, does not matter to the soul. But not understanding the mind and how it functions constantly creates problems because the mind builds a wall between the individual and the absolute Reality.

One should learn about his individual mind, about his thinking process. If he comes in contact with something depressing, undesirable, or repressive, he should understand that there are other dimensions of the mind that are very healthy, very creative, and very helpful. He should not be disappointed. Each person is fully equipped with all the instruments—body, senses, mind, and consciousness. To understand the nature of these tools means to attain the goal of life. This goal is actually not to search for God as religionists do. The real aim of Vedanta is to attain happiness, bliss, and wisdom. Happiness means freedom from all pains and miseries, and the greatest of all miseries is ignorance. The total absence of ignorance is a state of happiness. The goal of human life is to attain that state of happiness which is freedom from ignorance.

Wise people seek that ultimate knowledge, which is Truth or absolute Reality, so that they can attain the purpose of life.

After attaining that state of happiness, there is nothing else to be known. Where is the necessity for God in human life? Why does anyone need God? People say, "I need God, I want to see God." They create a serious problem for themselves by wanting to see God without understanding what God is. If someone repeats the word "God" again and again the whole day, it does not do him any good. People suffer on account of self-created miseries and then put the blame on God. Vedanta philosophy is a philosophy of actualism and realism, which views life logically.

The Upanishads, the finest of all books on this subject, say that Self-realization alone makes one free. When the student of Vedanta enters into an internal dialogue having the aim of Self-realization, he finds that purification of internal states is very important. He then understands that the actual need of life is to attain perfect happiness, peace, and bliss. This leads him to realize that faith has a place in life, but the faith that has not been filtered by the pure reasonings of higher buddhi is injurious and thus creates illusion and leads one to the darkness of ignorance.

In the path of knowledge, blind faith is completely shunned. Know, analyze, and then realize. By realizing the Truth, faith comes of itself. Such a faith can never mislead one. In the path of jnana yoga, all dimensions of life, within and without, are examined carefully by the intellect, which has been purified. The discriminative faculty of the buddhi is sharpened and strengthened. The external world and its objects are examined by this faculty of discrimination. The mortality of the objects of the external world is understood thoroughly. Such a student lives in the world, and the world is like a camp on the journey to enlightenment.

No one seems to be comfortable with oneself or with

others. The technique of living and being, the real art of happiness, seems to be lost in the midst of the charms and temptations of the external world. The external world poses a great threat to students, for it distracts their attention. In the path of jnana yoga, the scriptures declare that mortality and immortality are two different aspects of life and the universe. They should be understood thoroughly. Without understanding both of these aspects, one cannot progress. After careful study of the objects and forms of the external world, the student comes to know that anything that happens in the external world has already happened long before in the inner world. Therefore, his entire attention is focused on understanding his inner world. All human expressions depend on the thinking process. People act the way they think. Action is literally a thought form. The world of thoughts is enormously vast and is more subtle than the world of objects. Every human being has two avenues to express his feelings and thoughts: action and speech. These avenues have limited capacity to express the inner feelings.

Mind is conditioned by time, space, and causation, so the knowledge that is expressed through action and speech also has limitations. The mind is one of the finer instruments of the antahkarana—inner functionings. It is not possible for anyone to accomplish anything without it. In the path of jnana yoga the antahkarana is understood before the voyage is undertaken.

Inner Functions

A human being is like a complex factory, and each faculty of the mind has a specific job. There are four important functions or faculties of the mind: *manas, buddhi, chitta,* and *ahankara.*

Manas has a dual role. It functions both within and without. It is like that agent who has the responsibility of importing and exporting according to the need of the factory. It has the responsibility of collecting data and of expressing the inner feelings and thoughts to the external world. This faculty plays an important role; therefore it needs careful attention and training. It is this faculty that expresses the inner feelings and thoughts, with the help of ten subordinate workers—the five subtle senses (seeing, smelling, tasting, hearing, touching) and the five gross senses (mouth, hands, feet, and the two organs of elimination). It is manas who more or less directly guides the senses; the function of the senses depends on the mind.

Another faculty is called *buddhi*—pure intellect. This faculty is like an advisor in the factory of inner life, who directs manas (mind) to use its subordinates. This faculty discriminates, judges, and is responsible for all decisions. For lack of training, this faculty misleads the manas, and then the senses do not perform their duty accurately. When manas is trained to listen to the faculty of buddhi—intellect—peace of mind is attained. If manas and buddhi disagree or if the manas does not listen to the direction given by the buddhi, there will be no success in any field of life. An untrained buddhi and manas are the worst enemies one can have. In their disagreements, conflicts are created, and the more conflicts there are within, the more conflicts are reflected outside. Conflicts within and without are sources of human misery. They are self-created. These self-created miseries can be dispelled only when buddhi and manas are trained to function in a coordinated manner. Most people do not understand the importance of inner counseling, and for lack of inner counseling they cannot decide to do things on time. Lack of decisiveness is a great barrier. When one learns the method of inner counseling, he knows the way of knowing the other faculties, which are equally significant and play important roles in our inner lives.

We all talk about peace of mind, calmness, and tranquility, and we try to attain these states by acquiring external objects, but external objects have no capacity to give peace of mind or tranquility. They can only furnish certain comforts in the external world. If one is able to manage the affairs of the external world so that the external world no longer remains a source of distraction for the mind, that is a great achievement. The senses, which are used as avenues by the mind, definitely help one in conducting his duties in the external world, but without knowing the technique of controlling them, they are capable of disturbing peace of mind and creating mental imbalances. These senses are like the horses of a chariot; manas is like the driver; and the individual soul is seated behind. As untrained horses do not trod on the path, but always go here and there, so is the case with undisciplined senses, which are a source of conflict.

There is another faculty of our inner body that is called *chitta,* the storehouse of knowledge, memories, *samskaras,* and impressions. Though the center of Consciousness is beyond chitta, consciousness flows through chitta to the mind and then to the senses. It is important to understand the nature of the senses and the way they dissipate the energy of mind. When we talk of mind control or cultivating a peaceful and tranquil mind, we cannot ignore these avenues, which are constantly used by the mind. Chitta is not the individual soul, but the consciousness of the individual soul flows through chitta. It reflects the light of the soul. No human being ever looks at the sun when he walks, but he uses the light of the sun to see where he is going. In the same way, we do not have to look for the soul, but by being aware of the obstructions that prevent the knowledge of consciousness, we come to know that chitta is a storehouse of knowledge, but not the center. All the impressions received through our senses ultimately go to this storehouse through our nervous system, brain, and conscious mind. That enables us to remember the objects we have seen before. It is a vast reservoir of unlimited impressions having many levels.

The student of jnana yoga, with constant contemplation, learns to cross all the levels of the unconscious and enter into the world of light. The Upanishads explain that "the face of Truth is covered by a golden disc." This means that the glittering charms and temptations of the world dissipate the energy of the mind and senses and do not allow one to realize the Truth, which is veiled by the golden disc.

There is another faculty of our inner life that is called *ahankara,* the sense of I, that always lets one identify with that which is not realized. This is also called ego. It is that aspect of the mind which creates individuality. The strong sense of I-ness, that which separates one from the whole, is called ahankara. It is in the habit of building a boundary around itself and isolating itself from the whole. The ego works like the chief advisor or manager of the factory of inner functionings. It falsely claims itself to be the proprietor of the inner factory of life, forgetting the real proprietor, Atman. If the ego is not made aware of its source of strength, Atman, the center of Consciousness, it is called the lower ego. The lower ego is the greatest of all barriers. It does not allow one to see the real light, it always wants to retain individuality. The sense of individuality makes one feel small and petty. When the lower ego is carefully purified by constant contemplation on Atman, then that purified ego starts serving the purpose of fulfillment. Such a purified ego is a means. Without the help of ego, it is not possible to retain the individual body. If the nature of the individual ego is transformed, the ego becomes an instrument of awareness. It is said that the shortest way to realize the Self is just to train the ego. And one who is able to do this accomplishes the goal of life.

In the external world we notice that the improper use of ego creates many stumbling blocks for those who have never tried to train it. An egotistical person does not communicate well, and no one can communicate with him. In fact, many of us remain in the fortress of ego built by our egocentric whims.

In the path of jnana yoga all the faculties of our inner life are trained and guided to the center of Consciousness—*atma jnana*. The individual soul suffers because of its ego. It is just like appointing a dishonest manager in a business corporation. In the inner factory of life, the untrained ego, mind, and other faculties produce bad products. All the fancies, fantasies, sicknesses, and turmoils are because of the inner functions of human life.

It is antahkarana that stands like a barrier between the aspirant and the Truth. In order to train and purify all the functions or modifications of the mind, the aspirant learns to light the fire of knowledge for removing all the impurities of antahkarana. Through knowledge alone, absolute Truth is attained, and Truth alone liberates.

External Knowledge and Knowledge Beyond

The Upanishadic literature is full of dialogues and discussions on inner life and on the way one can attain the highest state of wisdom. These dialogues take place between two characters: *srotriyam brahmanistham*—the perfected one, the competent teacher—and the prepared one, called the disciple. These dialogues are not ordinarily understood by aspirants because they do not prepare themselves for such a quality of knowledge, which is beyond the grasp of senses, mind, and intellect. There are many levels of knowledge but two seem to be very important: *para vidya* and *apara vidya*. *Para vidya* means "the knowledge beyond," and *apara vidya* means "the knowledge of the external"—the knowledge of the unknown and the knowledge of the known; the knowledge of the abstract, and concrete knowledge. The world of objects, which is subject to sense perception, is called apara vidya, and that which cannot be grasped by external resources, senses, and mind, is called para vidya. How do we receive para vidya?

When one learns to direct all his energy inward and then to purify all the internal organs—internal states—he then receives the finest quality of knowledge from the infinite library already lying dormant within himself. Intuitive knowledge is that knowledge which does not need any verification or evidence for its validity. Such a pure knowledge removes the doubts of the aspirant and leads him to the fountain of consciousness within. Without gaining intuitive knowledge one cannot attain para vidya. *Para* means "beyond," and "beyond" here means "within." Mind is beyond the senses, the unconscious is beyond the conscious mind, and the individual Atman is beyond the unconscious; it is pure and self-illumined, having the essential nature of peace, happiness, and bliss. When the individual soul becomes aware of its universal nature, it realizes its ultimate goal. Self-realization is the goal of the aspirant, according to jnana yoga. In the process of Self-realization there are three main stages: first, I am Thine; second, Thou art mine; and third, we are one. The experience of unity in diversity is accomplished systematically through the path of knowledge.

Buddhi, having the faculty of discrimination, is carefully sharpened and purified. Such a buddhi turns within to fathom the deeper levels of life. During this voyage the buddhi goes through a period of argumentation and self-examinination. The aspirant starts examining everything. This period lasts until contemplation is strengthened. It is very natural for the individual to examine life on all levels, within and without, and to remove the subtle doubts that lurk in the unconscious.

In the path of jnana yoga, first a student practices an entirely different process of learning, and it is called the unlearning process. It is like programming oneself to completely unlearn. In this process one does not believe or disbelieve, condemn or accept any tradition or religion, without examining it. It is said that an atheist is better than a blind believer or follower of religion. Following beliefs without examining is to close the door of learning. An atheist is far superior to a person who blindly believes in God. An atheist wants to understand and know Truth, but a believer believes without understanding. We find two categories of people who believe in God. One is insecure, incompetent, ignorant, and fearful, and thinks that God, the highest being, will help him and guide him by becoming a savior. Another category includes people who are afraid because of the concepts of the devil and hell. Those who cannot face the problems of life, which are mostly self-created, go to the church, temple, or mosque with the idea that God will forgive them and make them happy. Such people find some solace and always use God for their convenience, but they are unable to build that sound philosophy which helps them understand life, with its currents and crosscurrents. To develop a sound philosophy one needs to have a free mind, free from the prejudices and influence of dogmas and doctrines.

The Major Questions of Life

The aim of human life for every individual is to directly experience the Truth. Such a direct experience gives birth to real faith and is accepted by the path of jnana yoga. Without having direct and profound knowledge of the Truth, one cannot have faith in it, and if he has, it will be partial. No religion is able to answer the vital questions of life: Who am I? From where have I come? What is the purpose of my life here? Where will I go from here? No religion answers these questions logically. These questions can only be answered by a philosophy that has been built with the sincere effort of contemplation. The promises of the scriptures do not satisfy the intellect of a seeker unless he knows for himself, and knows that he knows. The human mind, if not fully convinced, creates a serious threat to the aspirant in establishing a secure way of life. Every individual, by having direct experience, can convince the mind and remove its doubts. For an intellectual, these four questions always create riddles. The path of jnana yoga deals with the questions in a very rational way.

The first question—Who am I?—is the main question, and if one is able to find the answer, then he can understand, know, and receive the answers for the other questions. No matter which religious background one has, whatever tradition he follows, he has a strong and deep desire to know himself. All the creatures of the world have the same appetites: food, sleep, sex, and self-preservation. As far as these appetites are concerned, a human being is like an animal. The difference is that the life of animals is completely controlled by nature. They do not have intelligence, will power, and the method of knowing and discriminating between truth and that which is not truth. But a human being is capable of knowing, understanding, judging, and discriminating. He also has free will. Thus, the animal is not equipped the way a human being is. Human beings have the means to realize the goal of life. "Who am I?" is a question that can be answered by following the path of jnana yoga.

The path of jnana yoga explains that in the rotating wheel of human evolution, human beings can attain the highest status. If one examines the kingdoms of matter, vegetables, animals, and human beings, one finds that the human kingdom is highly evolved. The religious scriptures also accept that human beings are made in the image of God. But Vedanta philosophy says that a human being is the creator of his destiny and is the architect of his life. "Who am I?"—I am that Truth which cannot be separated by any power whatsoever. All the Bibles of the great religions of the world accept God as omnipresent, omniscient, and omnipotent power. Then where are we? Where do we exist? Is our existence a separate entity from the existence of the omnipresent? Who created us and what is the purpose of this creation? In the world we find miseries, pain, and suffering. Why should the omnipresent, omnipotent, and omniscient God create such a miserable world? The religions insist that we have to believe the sayings of the scriptures, and some of the religions even force us to believe what is written in their scriptures by creating the fear of the devil and evil. Is this not the way of destroying human intelligence? What good is a religion that does not allow one to think freely and that propagates the philosophy of fear? The path of jnana yoga declares that no power has ever created this universe or the dwellers and creatures of this universe; this is the manifestation of the one absolute Truth, without second. There is unity in diversity. Apparently, all the objects of the world seem to be different; they have different names, forms, and qualities. But essentially there is only one underlying principle of unity. Because of *maya,* the cosmic wheel, the human being remains in the darkness of ignorance. Maya is an illusion without any existence of its own. It is capable of creating apparent reality, but it has no existence of its own. Therefore, it is not absolute Reality. As darkness is lack of light, so ignorance is lack of knowledge.

By studying life, within and without, one can unveil the mysteries of maya and become free from the illusion that creates multi-dimensional confusion. The aspirant gets freedom by following the Vedantic way of life: "Not this, not this, not this." This path is called the path of negation, which means that the factual world of objects, having name and form, constantly changes, and thus cannot be considered Truth, because Truth is external and unchangeable all the time. The absolute Truth is self-existent and is hidden by the glittering veil of the charms and temptations of the world. Those who are able to remove that veil can realize the Truth.

Direct and Indirect Knowledge

The Upanishads, being the source of this knowledge, explain a definite way of Self-realization. It is important that the student of jnana yoga first listen to the scriptures, which are called *shruti*. The knowledge therein is direct knowledge attained by the great sages in deep contemplation. These sages devoted their entire lives to attaining this knowledge. *Shruti* and *smriti* are two sources of knowledge—direct and indirect, accordingly. Direct knowledge of the absolute is the highest quality of knowledge, coming through the intuitive library of the external. The Upanishads explain that there is only one absolute Truth, without second. Human beings and all the forms and names of the world are manifestations of that absolute Truth. Suffering, misery, and ignorance exist because of cosmic illusion.

The philosophy of the Upanishads leads the student through a systematic way of contemplation by imparting four *mahavakyas:* (1) Brahman alone is Truth, and the world of forms and names is false. The individual Atman and absolute Truth are one and the same; (2) There is only one Truth, without second; (3) This is all Brahman; (4) I am Brahman. These four mahavakyas are not mere Sanskrit words but indicate different states of realization. When a student has understood that the world of forms and names is false because it does not exist of its own, and that Brahman alone is Truth, then he attains the next step that there is only one absolute Truth, which exists everywhere. In the next state he realizes that his individual self and Brahman are one and the same. And finally, he realizes that he is Brahman.

After *mahavakya diksha*—knowledge of the great sayings of the Upanishads—the *brahmanistham,* or guru, explains the Upanishads, which are called shrutis. Shrutis are the direct revelations, and they are explained to the student by the teacher. The Upanishadic literature and other *sutras,*—such as the Brahma Sutras, and the gospel of fearlessness, the Bhagavad Gita—explain all the paths.

When the student attentively and devotedly listens to the teacher and the various commentaries of these scriptures, then he starts contemplating on the shrutis. One of the shrutis declares that "absolute Truth cannot be attained by studying the Upanishadic scriptures and by being a great intellectual." This means that the literature provokes the mind and intellect of the student to contemplate and have direct experience. Direct experience alone is the leader in the path of jnana yoga. This is a path that makes one fearless and releases one from the bonds of miseries and ignorance.

How does the aspirant contemplate according to this path? He contemplates on the sayings of the Upanishads, which lead him to realize that the human body is like a shrine and the indweller, Atman, is to be contemplated upon. In this path, no particular object or point of concentration is recommended. After some time the buddhi, or pure reason, starts flowing to the subtlemost levels of life—from *sravana,* or the hearing of the sacred texts from a competent guru, to *manana,* or contemplation on their importance, to *nididhyasana,* or meditation on the truth enshrined in them, and then finally to *satchitananda,* or pure existence, knowledge, and bliss.

This infinite vessel of life carries infinity within—and yet human beings are deprived of enlightenment? It is for lack of awareness that human beings suffer. When one learns to contemplate constantly on the eternal truth, he attains final liberation. A liberated and enlightened being knows that his Atman and Brahman are one and the same, and his essential nature is truth, bliss, and beauty—*"satyam, shivam, sundaram."* A human being is like a wave of bliss that arises from the ocean of bliss, all the time lives in it, and is an inseparable part of the ocean. From the unmanifested, he comes through manifestation, and then goes back to his original source.

All the forms and names of this world return to their original state from where they have come. There is no death for eternity; therefore, there is no death for Atman. That which changes and dies is the mortal part of the self, but immortality is free from change, death, and decay. It is the everlasting, unchangeable, and absolute Reality. The path of jnana yoga is mostly practical for renunciates, who have renounced the sense of "mine and thine" and who do not possess anything for themselves. The self of a renunciate becomes the Self of all.

In this path some practice only nonattachment, and live in the world and yet out of it. Others choose to renounce all attachments and pleasures. Desirelessness is the keynote for renunciates. There remains only one desire to be fulfilled, and that is the desire for Self-realization. Renunciates finally renounce even the desire for studying the scriptures and contemplating. When the aspirant finds water everywhere, he does not go to dig a well. Such a great master is called *brahmanistham.* A master who has crossed all the mire of delusion has become one with the Brahman. A drop of water and a river become the ocean when they meet the ocean. This is expansion and not the loss of individuality. When an individual expands his consciousness, he realizes universal consciousness. This freedom is called enlightenment, perfection, or *moksha.*

Chapter 3

Bhakti Yoga

The Path of Love and Devotion

Bhakti yoga is known as the path of love and devotion. It is the path of self-surrender and dedication of all one's resources to attain the ultimate Reality. In this path love becomes the Lord of life and motivates the whole being toward Divinity alone. The path of bhakti yoga is the path of love. This sounds so exciting to modern young people, that many want to follow this path, but only a few know what it really is. Many think that performing rituals and becoming fanatical makes one a follower of this path, and they also think that it is the easiest to follow. But it is not at all like that. Performing certain rituals to worship God is an easy way to keep the mind busy, but it is an inferior type of worship yielding no results and no progress in spirituality. In the higher way of bhakti, one totally surrenders everything to the Lord. The offering is not just a flower or a fruit, but all of oneself. There are no rituals involved. The offering is the devotee himself. He completely surrenders himself to the Divine.

Bhakti is a compound of two qualities: love and reverence. Love without reverence cannot be called bhakti. Reverence is also essential in human relationships. If one does not respect the person he loves, then there is something wrong with that relationship; that is not love. One cannot exclude love from reverence. There is a Persian poem that says, "On the ladder of love, reverence is the first rung leading to the person you love." If a person has no reverence for the beloved one, then he does not have true love.

One should also learn to love with one-pointedness. One-pointed love and reverence is called self-surrender. One cannot be selfish and egotistical and loving at the same time. If one is not giving and selfless, he can never follow the path of love. Bhakti means unconditional love, directing all the energies of mind, action, and speech for God only. Love for God is something different from love for human beings. Bhakti is love for God. It is a path of the heart and not of the mind.

The path of the heart is not mere emotionalism or sentimentality. If a person just allows whatever emotions arise to come into action without properly channeling them, the goal of life will remain unattained. One must learn to control that emotional power and channel it toward spirituality. Emotions are of two varieties: one is negative and the other is positive. When a negative emotion arises, one is distressed and becomes passive, depressed, or imbalanced. This is not control; this is being helplessly tossed about by an emotional outburst. But when a positive emotion arises, it makes one calm, joyous, and happy. The emotional body is like a fish tossed by the currents in the lake of the mind. If the mind is agitated by unfulfilled wants and desires, the emotional body is also disturbed; but when the mind is calm, the emotional body functions properly. Emotional maturity comes when one starts guiding his emotional powers consciously for creative use. In the path of bhakti, the devotee learns to tap that emotional force within and to control it properly so that it is channeled positively in one-pointed devotion for the Lord. He does not suppress his emotions, but intensifies them and directs them toward God.

The power of emotion is one of the highest of powers, and if directed properly, it leads one to the highest state of ecstasy. Many sages have known how to use this power for attaining *bhava samadhi*—the state of ecstasy that is one of the goals of the students of bhakti yoga. But if one does not know how to channel his emotions properly, he is not able to properly conduct himself because his mind creates obstacles. Disorganized emotions can even lead to insanity. Emotional problems are more serious than problems of the physical body.

Emotions arise from the depths of the lake of mind. A vast part of the mind remains buried within; this is called the unconscious mind. It is the unconscious part of the mind that motivates our behavior and governs our daily life. All the desires that have been repressed and suppressed are stored in the unconscious, and although we do not remain aware of these thought patterns or emotions, they exist. We have to learn to understand and to control these emotions. There is nothing in human life that cannot be brought under control. Control does not mean suppression; it means knowing how to use the emotions and to direct them properly. One should have conscious control over all his thoughts and emotions when he performs some action. Emotion arises from relationship with some person or object—emotion and relationship are interconnected. So if one wants to have emotional maturity, he should have understanding in his relationships.

The Source of Emotions: Four Primitive Fountains

All our actions are dependent on thought, all our thoughts are dependent on emotions, all our emotions are dependent on desires, and all the desires are dependent on four primitive fountains or innate urges that all human beings share. These are food, sex, sleep, and self-preservation. These four primitive fountains control the activities of all the creatures of the world.

Animals and human beings are equally motivated by these four urges, but human beings have the ability and means to establish orderly control over these four fountains. In dealing with any emotional problem, one has to analyze these four urges because all emotions arise from them. One thought form alone cannot be the source of emotions; it goes deeper than that. First, one should learn to study the four primitive urges and determine which has the most impact on his life, which controls his life. One of the greatest of all human agonies is not to be able to understand the primitive fountains and their impact on the human body and mind. When one learns to train his will and then uses it to control the four fountains, there is no question of "Don't do this," or "You have to do that." Whatever one does, he does with full control. In the modern world there is enough food, enough time to sleep and to enjoy things, but people do not seem to have the capacity or ability to make correct use of the objects of the world. They have no inner strength because they do not know how to regulate their emotional lives by regulating their appetites. Those who want to be powerful and creative in the external world, those who want to use their emotional power for enlightenment to attain the goal of human life, should learn to work on regulating the four appetites. One can easily learn to guide his emotional power by understanding his needs.

The first fountain is food. Many people overeat. One reason for that is that they are not supplying the proper diet to their bodies. The body is demanding certain nutrients and the person is not supplying them, so he overeats. Or, if one is supplying a nutritious diet, he may not be chewing his food properly, and so he is not allowing his body to absorb the nutrients. Many people prepare nutritious food, but they never take time to chew it properly. If one learns to chew his food properly, instead of gaining weight he will lose it.

Sometimes people overeat because they are frustrated.

Suppose one's sexual desire is unfulfilled. Quietly at night, he may slip to the refrigerator, eat, and then go back to sleep. People overeat unconsciously; there is a lack of awareness. The habit is slowly strengthened and eventually becomes unconscious. Then the person loses control and becomes helpless. So one should learn what to eat, when to eat, and how to eat, and he should regulate that urge by forming good eating habits.

A person's eating habits are entirely different from his sexual habits, but the two are interrelated. Food is given to the body first and then it affects the mind, but sexual desire comes to the mind first and then is expressed through the body. Suppose a man goes to sleep and dreams that he does sex. In the morning, if his wife awakens him and asks, "Would you like to do sex?" He might say, "No, I have already done it." But suppose he eats delicious food during a dream, and somebody awakens him and says, "Would you like to eat?" He would say, "Yes, I am very hungry." So there is a vast difference. Sex affects the mind first and then reflects on the body, but food is given to the body first and then affects the mind.

If one is insecure in his life, if he worries about what will happen to him next, then he might try to compensate. For example, as a substitute for this constant worrying he may become preoccupied and obsessed with sex. If he continues to allow these thoughts to be strengthened, they can disturb him. One should learn to regulate and channel that urge properly. Both extremes—brooding on sexuality all the time or repressing sexual desires—are unhealthy for the emotional life.

In the animal kingdom, the sexual urge is controlled by nature, while in the human kingdom, the sexual urge depends on the free will of the human being. This urge can be regulated, and thus imbalance arising from excessiveness can be avoided. Yogis regulate this urge by practicing the method of *urdhva retas* (upward traveling). This is a rare method of recycling the semen.

Such a yogi always enjoys good health and is never tossed about by the sexual urge. Excessive sexuality is a disease and a waste of time and energy.

Everyone wants to be joyous, but do they know which is the highest of all earthly joys? Many people would say sex, but when one is tired of doing sex excessively, what does he do? He wants to take rest and go to sleep. Sleep is actually the highest of all the restful joys for most people. But anyone who is conscientious in doing selfless service to humanity, who knows how to do his duty skillfully, and who works hard, does not need long hours of sleep. That selfless service becomes a prominent part of his life and gives him joy. Mahatma Gandhi slept for only two and a half hours a day, and yogis sleep only two and a half hours in twenty-four hours' time. Long hours of sleep do not necessarily give rest to the totality of one's being. When one wakes up after a long sleep he may find that he still feels tired because he did not get perfect rest. A person is not properly rested even if doctors give him anesthesia or if he takes sleeping pills to put him into deep sleep.

The anatomy of sleep is very complex. It is related to both the conscious and unconscious mind. The conscious mind is that part of mind that functions during the waking state. When it becomes tired because of the pressures and fatigue from the external world and the thought patterns and memories already stored in the unconscious, the senses do not coordinate and they refuse to function accordingly. Mental capacity and physical capacity are related. When the body and the conscious mind are tired, the unconscious mind helps them to take rest, and the necessity of sleep arises. Sleep is supposed to give rest to both the body and mind but very few know the technique of going to deep sleep by using their *sankalpa shakti,* or will power. The anatomy of sleep is hardly understood in this way, and human beings therefore do not derive enough benefit from this natural phenomenon. Let us remember that sleep gives only partial rest and never makes anyone wise. When a student learns to regulate this natural appetite, he can control the slothful tendency of his mind and utilize his time for higher purposes.

One should learn to take conscious rest, to go to sleep voluntarily. One can train himself, just as he can regulate his food and sex appetites, to sleep voluntarily and to wake whenever he wants. Yogis know the technique of going to deep sleep and rising at the exact time they want. This is called *yoga nidra*. In this technique, sankalpa shakti, a prominent aspect of will power, is trained to help one to have control over sleep. If one builds his will power by training the faculty of determination and says to himself, "I have to wake up in the morning at four o'clock," he will definitely wake up. But a long and deep-rooted habit of sloth comes in the way of strengthening will power. With the help of constant practice, one can break the old habit patterns and transform the personality. It is practice that makes one perfect.

Food, sex, and sleep are powerful urges in the human being, but the strongest of the four urges is self-preservation. Freud was right in saying that sex dominates one's life, but he did not realize that the sense of self-preservation actually controls one's life. The reflex action, which is a part of self-preservation, is so strong that even when one knows he is not really going to be hurt, still he will react automatically to protect himself. People also try to protect themselves all the time in their relationships. They argue because they do not understand each others' language and have lost the art of communication. This is a result of the urge for self-preservation—they want to preserve their separate identities.

It is interesting to note that all creatures have a natural tendency to protect themselves. The urge of self-preservation is equally strong in both humans and animals. Because fear is one of the prominent aspects of this urge, it has a deeper impact on the human mind than any other urge. To be fearless is a great achievement. Fearlessness comes only when one realizes that there is only one life force, there is only one truth beneath all names and forms. Such knowledge is not easily assimilated in human minds, because it is mind that actually separates the individual from the whole. Through knowledge of the ultimate Truth, the urge of self-preservation can be controlled. The fear of death and dying is one of the deepest in the minds and hearts of the ignorant. To a yogi, death whispers her secrets and nothing remains unknown to him. Those who have overcome the fear of death by being constantly aware of the eternal Truth can control the urge of self-preservation. Knowledge alone dispels the darkness. Through knowledge of the immortal Self the yogi understands that life is eternal and death is just like changing a garment. It is not annihilation of the Self. Fearlessness is a state of mind that helps one to live happily in the world.

The Seven Streams of Emotion

There are seven main streams of emotion that flow from these four primitive fountains. These are different from the urges in their quality and intensity, although they arise from the urges. Anyone who knows how to regulate these four urges, who knows how to control and direct them, can easily regulate these seven streams so that they will never flood their banks. These seven streams are *kama,* desire; *moha,* attachment; *ahankara,* egoism; *krodha,* anger; *matsarya,* jealousy; *mada,* pride; and *lobha,* greed.

The strongest of these streams is *kama,* the prime desire which is the mother of all desires. There are many different kinds of desires, and there are also vast differences in the levels of desires. If one does not know how to sort out and choose which desires are to be given expression, his life will be disastrous. People have innumerable desires, and they waste their time and energy fulfilling them. Kama is the prime desire that is the source of all motivations. It completely controls the life of all creatures. Under its influence one wants to have things for himself. It is desire, which, if not properly examined, can be disastrous. The desire for objects, experiences, and feelings related to the mind and the senses is the source of pain and suffering in this world. But if desire can be channeled properly, then it can lead to success.

The next emotional stream is *moha*—attachment. Desire is the mother, attachment is the father, and they go on breeding. Attachment is the greatest monster in the history of mankind that misguides and destroys the creative potentials of human life. It is like intoxication. Under its influence one becomes like "a drunken monkey stung by a scorpion." Almost everyone has the desire to remain attached to something. When one is attached to something, he is even willing to sacrifice himself for the sake of his attachment. But attachment and love are totally different. If someone loves someone wholeheartedly, he will always remain detached and serve the loved one selflessly without wanting to receive any fruits therefrom. Wants and desires cause misery and are the very basis of attachment. While love gives freedom, attachment makes one blind and robs the power of reasoning. Love expands, but attachment contracts and causes many problems. Attachment should be modified into love. Love means giving with no expectation, and that expands con- sciousness. In attachment, however, one becomes selfish and has expectations all the time. One can live in the world and love all the things of the world, but he must remember that they are not his and that he has no right to be attached to them. The world is full of charms and temptations; that is why it is so distracting.

Attachment is based on ego—*ahankara*. Most people think that the ego is bad, but this is not so. Ego creates a barrier only when one does not know how to use it. It is a power that is good if one knows how, where, and when to use it. The ego helps people by creating a defense mechanism to protect them. It is an important part of life as far as the external world is concerned, but it should not be misused; it should not be fed with worldly thoughts and possessions all the time.

Ego has two aspects: higher and lower. The lower ego makes one petty and egocentric. It separates one from the whole, but the higher ego is helpful in expanding one's consciousness. The lower ego remains arrested with a sense of individuality—"this is I." When one has such an ego problem, he creates a block and does not communicate with others. The more egotistical one is, the more isolated and lonely he is. But when one starts understanding that underneath "you and me" there is only one principle of equanimity and oneness, then one will start loving others instead of being a victim of the lower ego. He will stop creating a boundary. When the ego is purified, it loses its lower quality and becomes the higher ego. The lower ego is a barrier, a hindrance, but the higher ego is an instrument, a means.

The lower ego can be trained and used to become a higher ego. This is done by self-surrender. It is good for one to surrender, but one should never surrender himself before the temptations of the world, or he will be disappointed. What is the right way of surrendering? Surrendering before God, before Reality, before Truth, is the right way of surrendering. This means accepting Truth with mind, action, and speech. When one surrenders oneself to the loved one, there is no longer a sense of individuality that acts as a barrier, and the ego is used as a tool to serve humanity. Exactly as a drop of water meets the ocean, the highest individual expands himself to cosmic Consciousness.

Anger is another stream of emotion. Anger means that someone has a suppressed or unfulfilled desire. If one cannot have what he wants, he feels insecure and frustrated. His anger affects those nearby immediately, and they react with anger to him. But if they could remain quiet and not react, then after a while the angry person would realize he had behaved irrationally, and he would not react foolishly and get angry again.

Anger can be converted by using patience as a positive weapon to defeat it. One should also learn to be patient with oneself and to practice the philosophy of nonviolence in his relationships.

Jealousy, another stream, is closely related to anger. If one doesn't have something that he wants and someone else has, then he feels jealous. Jealousy is very dangerous; it creates constant competition, and one always remains insecure. Pride is another stream. If one's desire is fulfilled and he becomes controlled by the sense that he has things and others do not, then that is pride. But if one has things and knows how to use them, then that is not pride. Greed is the stream of emotion in which one wants more and more of what one desires.

These emotional streams disturb the whole being and distract one from the path of unfoldment, but if he understands these streams and their functions, then he can analyze and understand himself. And if one learns how to channel these emotional streams for creative use, then he is victorious and can do wonders in life. We all know that these negative emotions are harmful and should be controlled. Although we know this, we cannot always live according to it. We know, and we know that we know, but we cannot live according to our knowing, and this is a source of frustration. Love alone is the great strength that can give us the capacity to live according to our knowing. Love alone has the power to change one's personality, but a weak human being is not capable of loving others. He does not have the strength to love because he is weak. Love is that source of inner strength that can transform all negative emotions into positive ones.

The Positive Expression of Emotion

People are always expressing their emotions in various ways—by talking, gesturing, chewing gum, driving fast, singing, dancing, painting—and it is always healthy for one to express himself in a positive way. A gentle man expresses himself in a positive way, and that is called virtue, but a criminal expresses himself in a negative way, and that is called crime. When one knows his own emotional life, then he can easily know others, and he can communicate with others and express himself positively. But people do not communicate with each other. They talk about love all the time, but they do not know themselves, so they cannot present themselves properly, and they are not able to understand others. People are lonely because they are not aware of the fountain of love within. They think that the objects of the world or other human beings have the capacity to make them happy, but alas, no person and no object can make anyone happy. Happiness lies within. People should learn to give up these expectations of others, to give, to express their emotions positively, and to communicate with others nicely. Chanting or singing is one of the finest ways of expressing one's emotions. Instead of shouting at one's spouse or children or pets, one can chant or sing. Music, dance, and art are creative ways of expressing one's emotions, and they can be very beneficial if they are used properly.

One can also let his emotions out through prayer, and it can even strengthen one's meditation if properly used. There are two sorts of prayer: ego-centered prayer and prayer of the divine. In ego-centered prayer a person puts personal, selfish demands before God. He says, "O God, I don't have this; I need that. Give me this, give me that." That is called ego-centered prayer. But the most beneficial prayer is that which comes from within. In inner prayer, one is not actually praying to someone else; he is becoming aware of the finest part of himself. He is praying to the Lord within who is the very summum bonum of life, who is the very source of one's life. In inner prayer, one says, "O Lord, I want strength so I can face all the problems of life. Grace me so that I have that strength."

A person should feel some deep meaning when he prays, or

else it is just mere speech and does not help. Prayer without faith is not helpful either, so one should learn to have faith in his prayers. Faith means that the mind does not intervene, and one's whole being flows with one-pointedness toward the beloved one. Faith is the leader in the path of bhakti. It is said that faith can move mountains, and it does. But most students who tread this path become victims of the fantasies and fancies of their minds and start hallucinating. Thus their progress is hampered. Such students even become imbalanced and cry whenever they listen to devotional songs or study the scriptures. On every path there are obstacles to overcome, and so is the case on the path of bhakti. If emotion is not guided carefully, one can lose his balance and become a victim of his illusions.

When one prays properly, his whole being is intense. Prayer is a method of soul-searching that purifies the way of the soul. In the path of bhakti one of the easiest practices is to remember God's name—a mantra or a word—constantly. *Ajapa japa,* remembering God's name constantly, becomes a part of life and makes one aware of the Lord all the time. Constant remembrance makes a deep groove in the unconscious mind, for the unconscious mind is actually the seat of habit formation. Once the habit is formed, then it becomes part of individual life. Ajapa japa is that state of remembering God's name in which a devotee does all his duties, yet remembers God all the time, even during sleep. It is an effortless way of remembering God, but a constant and long practice of japa is necessary. Those who have formed a habit of ajapa japa enjoy inner silence without any effort. They do their duties and remember the Lord's name all the time.

Prayer is the greatest source of inspiration and strength, provided one learns to pray wholeheartedly and does not make demands in his prayers. One should pray to his full capacity, and he should know that the highest of all powers is the power of love. I examined this for myself. Once I prayed for ten hours, but my internal state remained the same. I prayed feeling I was different from the Lord, with no results. Then I completely surrendered and said, "Lord, I am Thine and Thou art mine. I am a drop and you are the ocean. There is no place for me elsewhere but you." Then there came some courage from within, and that cloud of separation was dispelled. Between the inner Self and the person there lies a veil. In inner prayer, one removes that veil. Prayer is always answered; there is no doubt about it.

As prayer is one of the important aspects of bhakti yoga, meditation is important in raja yoga, contemplation in jnana yoga, and selfless service in karma yoga. Prayer purifies the way of the soul and prepares one for the higher steps of bhakti. In bhakti yoga, many students use an idol, an image, or a statue of a spiritual guide because their minds cannot fathom the attributeless aspect of the Lord. This way of ritual, or *puja,* that they perform helps to make the mind one-pointed and inward. The scriptures explain that there are two levels of devotion— devotion for the attributeless, and devotion with attributes (*nirguna* and *saguna*). It is not easy for a student to attain nirguna *bhava,* or mood, and it takes a long time for the student to attain nirguna bhakti. The human mind is accustomed to leaning on certain forms or names. It cannot conceive of and is not able to fathom the unfathomable—the attributeless. Therefore, very few attain nirguna bhakti, but saguna bhakti seems to be very easy and pleasing to the students of this path.

In the path of bhakti, a selfless and competent guide is needed so that one does not get distracted by the experiences of the mental world. Study of the scriptures, constant japa, and complete dedication and self-surrender are the very keys of this path. *Vairagya* (nonattachment) while doing one's duties, and always remembering the Lord with a feeling of self-surrender, are the keynotes of this path.

By understanding, analyzing, and directing the emotional power, one can become creative and successful in the world and attain the highest state of ecstasy. That highest state of consciousness dawns when one surrenders himself. Then he is like a flute. Although a flute has many holes, many imperfections, yet it plays. But if someone inserts something inside the flute, it will not play. A person says, "I have so many weaknesses." But he needn't worry. He is like a flute with many holes, which will play if one doesn't allow anything to remain inside. One needs to become an instrument of the Lord by making oneself empty, by purifying oneself. A purified soul is a messenger of God; he is a prophet of love who emanates love wherever he goes. A human being is an unfinished being. His completion is accomplished only when he becomes aware of the presence of the Lord in his daily life.

The student of bhakti yoga shouldn't condemn himself by saying, "I don't know anything. I don't have wisdom. I am ignorant. I am guilty. I am a sinner." One should not make himself suffer like that. He shouldn't condemn himself, for no one benefits from that. Self-condemnation leads to guilt feelings, and guilt feelings create psychosomatic disorders. There are teachers who through their preaching create guilt feelings in their followers. By creating fear they try to lead their followers toward Godhead, but what good is that religion which creates fear in the minds of human beings? The purpose of religion is to free its followers from fears. Many religious preachers intentionally create fears in the minds and hearts of their followers, but this is unhealthy and irreligious. Actually, sinners are those who preach religion to fulfill their own selfish goals. Many students who are not capable of judging what is right or wrong become victims of such preaching. Our society is full of such preachers and students. This religious sickness makes one a blind believer. Such preachers and followers condemn other paths without having any knowledge. There are many cults that are active in preaching religions that create fear and guilt in the minds and hearts of the people. There is not any path in spirituality that can be trodden without discipline, and for disciplining the student, creating guilt and fear is not helpful. There is no place for guilt in love, for love forgives all. There is always grace in love, and that grace is called forgiveness. When one commits a mistake, it is because he did not know any better at the time or was weak then. It does not mean he is a bad person because of it. One should not identify himself with his past actions, forgetting the totality of his personality. One's action is only his expression; it is not him. If it is wrong, he should just stop expressing it.

The Source of Positive Emotions— The Inborn Urge to Know God

The power of emotion arises from desires, and desires arise from the four primitive fountains, but there is another basic urge in human beings. This is the drive to know the Truth, the desire to love the Truth. This dormant inborn desire within does not arise from one of the four fountains. It is the source of positive emotions—joy, forgiveness, and peace. It is not possible for a human being to be free from desire, because it is the nature of the mind and the senses to be attracted to objects and ideas. This is not bad; it is a fact that can be used. Even that desire which is one's greatest burden can be a means for his liberation if he learns to direct it properly. When that force is directed toward the divine instead of toward the external charms and temptations of the world, then one's journey is propelled by the power of love, for love is the strongest force. One can use that natural tendency to desire something as a means for attaining the highest goal in life. When one does not allow his mind to be dissipated and agitated by the senses and the ego, then he finds that center of love within. When that spark is ignited, it becomes a burning desire to reside always in union with the Divinity. Then that great conflagration burns away all little desires, and there is only one perennial flame burning in the altar of the heart.

One has simply to surrender by accepting the higher Reality in daily life, and then enjoy. This is called *sadhana* in the world here and now. It is *bhava bhakti,* the power of love. That higher Reality is already within each of us. One has but to accept oneself and to know oneself to be one with that Reality. Real love means letting go of the familiar and the material and leaping into the endless wave of pure love for Truth. That love is the one great tidal wave that sweeps over all the little waves of distracting emotions in life. This is frightening to many because the mind wants to continue to act as it has been trained to be—dissipated and distracted. But this wave of one-pointed devotion is a wave of bliss and beauty that transforms a person. One has not to stop enjoying the world, but one can let whatever he does for pleasure become an act of worship, an offering to the Beloved. This is beautifully stated in Shankara's *Saundaryalahari:* "Through the act of self-surrender, let my prattle become recitation of your name, the movement of my limbs gestures of worship, my walk perambulation around you, my food sacrificial offering to you, my lying down prostration to you; whatever I do for my joy, let it become transformed into an act of worship to you."

There are positive powers within every human being, and the power of emotion is one of the highest. It can enlighten one if he learns to direct that force properly. Buddha said, "Learn to light thy own lamp. No one else can give you salvation." One simply has to know the light behind this lamp of light. There was a sage in Punjab whose name was Bulleshah. Someone once asked him, "Sir, tell me, how can I attain God?" He said, "Why are you bewildered? It is very easy to attain God. Simply disconnect yourself here," he said, pointing downward, "and connect yourself there"—pointing up. "Direct your emotions upward toward God and never forget these words: 'This body is like a shrine, and He who dwells within, that Light within, is the Bright Being in you. Know Him first!'"

To do this, one does not necessarily have to make any

changes in his daily life or withdraw from the world. Only one's attitudes toward life and toward the world should be changed. To find peace one need not run away, sit under a tree, or go live in a monastery or in the Himalayas. All the sages were not renunciates. Many of them lived in the world because they knew how to organize, how to control, and how to direct their energies. Anyone who is able to do that is free here and now. He remains above like a lotus, the symbol of yoga science. The lotus grows in the mud, in the water, but it keeps its petals free from the effects of the water and the mud. In the same way, a person of awareness learns how to live in the world yet remain above. A master is he who knows how to live in the world and yet remain unaffected by it. So one can live wherever he is, but he should learn to organize his actions, his thinking process, and his emotions. We human beings have that capacity, but it will not be realized as long as we limit ourselves to matter, energy, and mind. One has to learn to understand *bhava,* the power of emotion.

Bhava bhakti, the power of love, is essential for leading a joyous, meaningful, and creative life. It is easy to control and direct the emotions for creative use provided one has learned to be positive. Love is that force which we feel and understand, but cannot explain. Love is the most ancient traveler there is. When we examine the process of the human voyage, we come to know that when a child is born, its first love is for its mother's bosom; then it takes to love for dolls, and perhaps later there is love for gaudy colors. Then love develops for honors and certificates from colleges and universities, then love for the opposite sex, for one's children, and for self-respect. We think that these phases of love are very necessary, but when we examine them we find that many times we are just feeding our individuality. Finally, in old age, when one examines the whole process of his life, he finds that he has not attained anything worthwhile and is still unfulfilled. Then after one has given up having love for all the objects of the world, one begins to develop love for life, love for Truth, love for God, and finally, love without object. This is the purest, highest love of all.

Human hearts and minds need objects as centers for their love. Actually this is called love for objects, which ultimately leads one to sensuality and attachment. It is a sort of dependency that mind always finds for itself. Mind is in the habit of resting, focusing, and depending on an object. This sort of love makes one weak and dependent. True love dawns when one learns to love without an object. Love without an object is real bhakti; it is love for Brahman, the ultimate Reality.

Selflessness and Self-Surrender

Selfishness creates boundaries around human beings and makes them captive, petty, and small. Love is not a selfish gesture; love means being selfless. There are two principles that we see in our daily lives: the principle of contraction and the principle of expansion. To become selfish is to follow the principle of contraction, and to become selfless means to expand one's consciousness. When someone becomes very selfish, his personality is contracted, but if he would be completely selfless, he would find his consciousness expanding. When one becomes selfish he expects something. Generally in human relationships one expects something first and then love comes afterward. In the world, people expect much from each other. Most of the miseries that we find in the world are because of expectations. A wife expects her husband to love her, and her husband expects to be loved. This is expectation, and expectation is the mother of all problems. Expectation mingled with attachment brings all the miseries of the world. The wife expects too much from her husband, and the husband expects too much from his wife. They call this love, but they are actually obstructing their way of knowing truth. Love overcomes the problems created by the reasoning mind and the negative emotions and desires; love is the greatest solvent of all difficulties, all problems, all mis-understandings.

Many of us feel that it is not possible for one to learn and practice the path of bhakti or love. For practicing and learning to love, one should first learn to practice *ahimsa,* or non-harming. Ahimsa is the true expression of love. To practice bhakti, one has to practice ahimsa with one's mind, action, and speech. By expressing non-harming and non-injuring, one is practicing ahimsa. Ahimsa is so practical that one can easily apply it to cross this mire of delusion. One can go beyond and enjoy that perennial center of love. But this is not possible as long as expectation is the motivation in one's daily life. When expectation is not fulfilled, one gets frustrated, angry, and isolates himself and loses touch with the Reality.

To be loved means to love. Love means giving, giving, giving, where there is no thought of any return or reward. To give wholeheartedly and unconditionally is called love. One should learn to love without expectation, or if one cannot live without it, he should expect less and love more. One should not expect any reward from the beloved one. In the path of bhakti, one doesn't expect any rewards. He surrenders; he gives completely. When one gives completely, he has given up everything, and he gives everything. That is called love, self-surrender. And self-surrender is the highest of all yogas. As long as one has not surrendered his mere self to the highest Self, he cannot learn to love. One has to surrender himself. The principle is to give and to feel delight in giving.

In self-surrender an individual becomes an instrument of the Lord, and his mind, action, and speech become channels for the expression of bhakti. When the mind does not disturb, distract, and dissipate human potentials, then higher con-sciousness reveals itself through such a human being. Because of their unconditional love for God, the great sages performed impossible feats that cannot be analyzed. Unconditional love for God is the highest of all aspects of love. If human beings learn to express their divine love toward other human beings and creatures, they will establish heaven on earth.

Love is the very basis of renouncing selfishness. When one goes on renouncing, he will attain that state for which he longs. In the path of bhakti, *vairagya* (nonattachment) is natural and easy. As one's love for the Lord intensifies, attachment to all else simply falls away of its own accord. The path of bhakti is a spontaneous path, provided one has learned to surrender all that he possesses, owns, and thinks that he owns. A student of this path remains fearless always.

The Steps to Attainment

In the path of bhakti, one does everything for God; no importance is given to individuality. One does nothing for oneself. All things are offered to the Lord. But in the path of karma, one is doing his action for someone, relating through someone, to God. A husband is serving his spouse because she is a representative of God. Whatever one does for one's husband or wife, for one's children, neighbor, or humanity, one is doing for God. That is called the path of action. But in the path of bhakti, God alone comes first. In the path of bhakti, one surrenders all he has. He says, "My actions, my speech, my thinking, all that I have is Thine. I am Thine; Thou art mine." When one learns to direct his emotions, when he learns the positive power of emotion, when he actually learns to love, then he will always remember to surrender everything that he has. Anything one thinks is his, he will surrender, saying, "It is Thine, Thine, Thine!" A real devotee is he who silently gives all that he has. He doesn't wait for liberation to be attained in the next world, for he is liberated here.

There are three steps in bhakti. Bhakti is the path of the

student who believes in the philosophy of dualism. The first step is "I am Thine," and the second step is "Thou art mine." Then one starts identifying himself with the beloved Lord, and with one-pointed devotion he becomes one with the beloved Lord; he realizes that he and the Lord are one. These steps are not to be merely spoken about; they are to be realized. They are the steps of pure love for God. When Christ said, "I and my Father are one," he was in that state of oneness. And when he said, "This is not my power, this is the power of my Father. That is how I am healing you," he was in the state of "I am Thine."

Jesus trod the path of bhakti, and practical Christianity is the path of bhakti . The early Christians practiced this path, but Christians today do not practice it accordingly. Jesus Christ was born on the earth as a human being just as we are, and he proved that human beings have those qualities, those potentials, to attain a state of perfection. The philosophy of Jesus is the philosophy of love, of bhakti. He said that the greatest law of life is to love God with one's whole mind, heart, and spirit and to love one's neighbor as oneself. Jesus' closest disciple, John, said, "He who does not love does not know God, for God is love. . . . . He who abides in love abides in God, and God in him" (1 John 4:8, 16). Paul, who was transformed from a persecutor to a saint by the power of love, gives a beautiful description of love in one of his epistles. He says, "Love is always patient and kind; it is never jealous; love is never boastful or conceited, it is never rude or selfish, it does not take offense, and is not resentful. Love takes no pleasure in other peoples' mistakes and weaknesses but delights in the truth; it is always ready to forgive, to trust, to hope, and to endure whatever comes." Love is the eternal law of life. Christianity is based on this philosophy, and many Christian saints, such as Francis and Teresa, were great *bhaktas*. All religions teach the path of devotion, but most people do not know what it really is. When we understand the essential points of all great religions, we will come to know that they are one and the same. All the great religions have risen from the same center of love. They all say be loving, be kind, be gentle, be truthful. Where is the difference between religions? The difference lies in nonessentials. Most people think devotion means rituals and formulas, but the sages and mystics understood its true meaning, for they realized their union with Divinity, which mingles all the strains of joy and sorrow into the song of life.

In the path of bhakti, pain and pleasure lose their value. One goes beyond them, for he has surrendered everything. He says, "The way You want me to live, I will live. You are the creator of my destiny; why should I worry about it?" If complete self-surrender is missing, that is not called reverence, or love; that is not called bhakti. In the path of love, everything is self-surrender. Suffering has no place on such a path. Suffering is a joy in the path of love. One is so devoted that all his actions transform into that something which is called love. There is no pain, for he has accepted everything as love. If pain comes, it is a part of love. There is only love.

Real Bhaktas

Real bhaktas always have one-pointed devotion, reverence for the Beloved, and complete self-surrender. There is no want, there is no petition, there is no expectation. Bhakti leads one beyond pain and pleasure. For real bhaktas, everything is joy. They are like a river that rushes and sings, swings and jumps in joy when she flows from the mountains to the valleys of the Himalayas. She is chanting songs and dancing to meet the ocean, her Beloved.

But there are two types of lovers or bhaktas. One is called an actual lover, and the other is called a "milk-taker." There is a very interesting story about this that is based on a historical fact. There was once a princess named Laila and a poor boy named

Majanu. They studied in the same school, and they developed a deep love for one another. But because of their family status and duties, they could not marry. Instead of doing his lessons, that boy used to think of Laila all the time. The teacher would say, "Write God," and he would write Laila's name. The teacher would say, "Say God," and he would say, "Laila." He did not know anything in the world except Laila. He forgot even his own name and existence. He became lost in his love for Laila. Laila was a princess and lived in a palace. All his attention was focused on her, but Majanu stayed outside the city under a tree. It was not possible for the princess to get married to a boy like Majanu.

Majanu would never open his eyes to see anyone or anything. Laila would send milk to her lover in the dark of night by way of her maidservant. Another young man found out that milk was being sent to that imbalanced man, and he thought, "Why should I not pose as him and get some milk for myself? He won't see me." So that young man became a counterfeit lover. He sat down under a tree, and the maidservant mistakenly gave him the milk. He enjoyed it while the real Majanu suffered. God said, "That is not just. That is not fair." So He came down to test them both to find out who was true and who was not. God brought milk, appearing as a beautiful woman to attract and charm the two lovers, to find out who was the real lover. To the fake one he said, "I am Laila. I brought milk for you." The fake lover opened his eyes, and said, "Sweetheart, sit next to me." God said, "I want a cup of blood from your body," but the fake lover refused to give it. He said "I am only a milk-taker. Go to that man who is sitting under that tree." Then God went to the real lover for testing the intensity of his love, and said, "Here am I, your beloved." Majanu said, "No, you are not." Then God said, "I am God. Have a glimpse of me." Majanu said, "I don't have any desire to fill my eyes by seeing God." God said, "What are you saying? Nobody in this world could ever dare say such a thing!" But Majanu said, "If you are really God then you should know me. My God, my life, my everything is my Laila. Only for my Laila will I open my eyes. I don't want to see anyone else. My whole devotion is toward Laila. I don't need your sympathy. I don't need any heaven. I don't need anything from you. I don't need any God. I need my love of love, Laila."

God was pleased to see his one-pointed devotion, and even tried to tempt him. He said, "I will grant all boons to you. I will make you the king of the universe. Just stop saying her name, and accept me as God." Majanu said, "I don't care for anything, I don't want to become king of the universe." God was pleased to find that he was so selfless and devoted. Majanu said to God, "If you really want to do something for me, come to me as my Laila and not as God." (Similarly, the poet Tulsidas expressed such a desire to Lord Krishna. He said, "O Lord, if you want to bless me with your glimpse, appear before me as my Lord Rama.")

Majanu said, "My pain has crossed the boundaries of all joy. This whole universe is Laila for me. My love has expanded so much that it has become universal. This whole universe is my Laila. You cannot separate my love from the universe." From then on he would continually say, "Laila, Laila, Laila." This sort of love leads to *para bhakti,* the universal love.

The path of love is unique. It moves those who follow it to express their devotion in lyrical ecstasy. Many well-known poets and sages of the East—such as Surdasa, Tulsidas, and Kabir—were great bhaktas, great devotees of the Lord. A few centuries ago, one such poet, whose name was Meera, was a sublime example of bhakti. She is famous in the literary history of India for her devotion to the Lord Krishna.

She was a princess from Rajasthan, and she was fascinated by stories of Krishna from very early childhood. Once she met a holy man who carried the image of Krishna all the time. The young Meera begged the sage to give her the image of the Lord, but to her utter disappointment she did not get it. This broke her heart, and she forsook food and plunged into deep sorrow. On the third night the Lord appeared in the sage's dream, ordering him to give the image to Meera, so he did. Meera's love for the image grew deeper and deeper. She played with the image like a living playmate. She would talk to it and sleep with it.

One day as she watched a wedding party go by, she asked her mother who her groom would be. Meera's mother, fully aware of Meera's deep love and devotion to Krishna, jokingly told her that she would be married to Lord Krishna. That was the day Meera pledged her heart to her divine bridegroom, Lord Krishna. But later, Meera's parents forced her to get married to Prince Rana. When Meera went to live with her husband, her mind was not there, but all the time remembered Krishna. She would quietly slip out of the bridal chamber to worship the image of Krishna. Her slipping out of the palace all alone at night was not at all accepted by her in-laws, and false rumors about her started to spread. The family was enraged at the shame she was bringing upon them, and her husband and in-laws decided to kill her. One day while she was meditating on the image of Krishna, they sent a goblet of poison to her and asked her to drink. She never ate or drank anything without offering it to Lord Krishna, and after she offered the goblet of poison, she gladly drank it. To their amazement, the in-laws later saw that Meera was still alive, meditating, and merged in the devotion of Krishna. One day Meera decided to renounce her home and visit various shrines, composing songs of the Lord. These songs are sung even today by men and women in all walks of life. The matchless picture of Meera in the devotional literature of India will always be a symbol of pure devotion and bhakti for the Lord.

Becoming a real lover of God means directing one's love, directing one's emotions toward creative use. What is the sign of such a lover or bhakta? A real bhakta is one who has given everything to humanity, and once someone acquires such a taste, he cannot live without it. No matter how many times the world persecutes him, that persecution is a joy, and he lives happily, for he has gone beyond these relative terms. When Christ was crucified, he was the happiest person in the world because he was crucified for the sake of truth. One who is solely devoted to the Lord is always fearless. If one is wasting time in trying to eliminate physical pain, how can he get freedom from mental pain? We have to learn to be strong, and strength comes from within. The center of strength is the center of love. Those who are conscious only of their birth and their existence on this platform always remain afraid of so-called death. But it has been examined by the great sages of all times that death has no power to change human destiny. Only love has the power to change.

One should be free of the fear of death, and having attained this freedom he should direct his energies for the attainment of spirituality. The hallmark of spiritual greatness is selfless service. There is one common quality in all the great people of the world, though they have trodden various paths, and that is that they were all selfless. They did everything for the sake of others; they lived to serve others. Christ was so selfless that when he was crucified he never said, "I am in pain!" His conviction for love was so deep that he did not care about crucifixion. Moses, Buddha, Krishna and other spiritually great men were all very selfless. Their examples show us that love actually means renunciation of individual joys and nonattachment to the objects of joy. The highest of all states is called selfless love for others. After doing many, many experiments in life, one finally comes to realize, "Why am I doing this thing for myself? It should be done for others. Let others be happy." Then enjoyment comes because others are happy. When one has developed that sense, then he cannot stop loving people and helping them. Great are those who serve others selflessly. Through serving others they express their love. The scriptures say, "Knowing that the Lord is in every being, the wise have thus to manifest unswerving love toward all beings."

Great people are selfless in their love for humanity; but today, most world leaders are suffering on account of the cult of individuality and egoism. When one is egotistical, he reinforces the boundaries on which he has built his whole life by giving himself the feedback that "I exist." Then he is really strengthening his isolation, thinking he will be protected. But that kind of protection strangles human progress, and it does not allow humanity to improve, to attain the next step of civilization. There is only one power, and that is the power of love. Love is the center that radiates life and light, but humanity has not yet learned to understand what it is. If there will be one true religion in the future of mankind, it will be universal love.

A burning desire to know the Lord, to have union with the Lord, will remove all obstacles. The power of love is more powerful than any other force. It dissolves all obstacles and barriers and pours itself without limit to the Beloved. In the presence of complete surrender, the Divine pours itself without limit back into the creation. Love for the Divine brings one in touch with one's own divine nature. It is highly intoxicating, that nectar of love dripping like ambrosia from the heavens. It will not come automatically of itself, though. One has to put forth sincere effort and surrender himself fully. What good is it to pray, "O Lord, help me. I want to be with you!" The Lord cannot open the heart of the seeker or break the wall that separates them. The seeker must clear those barriers himself, for he is the one who has built them. Actually, the seeker is already with the Lord—it is the seeker who thinks he is alone. The Lord is waiting for the seeker to embrace Him. The seeker is not helpless; the Lord knows one's needs, and he gives everything to those who are prepared and deserving. One should make sincere, constant effort of one's own.

Love does not question, expect a reward, or doubt. It is always patient and giving and trusting. It endures no matter what comes, and it never thinks of itself. Real love is a silent inner bond that can never be broken. It is a deep understanding that requires no outward signs of reassurance from the Beloved, and yet it constantly expresses itself through selfless giving and surrender. If one simply dedicates his heart and mind and surrenders without expectation, then one receives the highest bliss.

Only those who are solely devoted to the Lord know the value of the path of bhakti. Those who do not know how to give, learn through practicing inner communication with the Divine and through acting on the guidance of their conscience. For most people, it helps at the beginning to select an image of the Divine on which to contemplate. People in different cultures use different manifestations such as Jesus, Krishna, or Buddha. Rituals of worship are made to focus the mind and channel the emotions, but the highest worship is beyond rituals and worship of images. It is inner worship—the direct silent communication with the Divinity within. This union can go on all the time, not just during meditation. That is what is meant by being in the world and yet remaining above. When the devotee attains this union, then every act is an act of worship and all of life is a song of love and bliss.

Chapter 4

Karma Yoga
The Path of Action and Selfless Service

Karma is the expression of the rule of perfect justice within us. It is the law of the cosmos reflected in the microcosm. There is nothing arbitrary or punitive about it. It is universal law and inevitable fact. No success can be attained without understanding the law of karma, and most of the human beings in this world follow the path of karma yoga consciously or unconsciously. Those who know that the path of karma is like worship of the Lord perform their actions skillfully, selflessly, and lovingly.

Many people are confused about the definition of karma. When something adverse happens, they say, "It's my karma." Actually, karma cannot be classified as good or bad. The word *karma* comes from the Sanskrit root *kri,* meaning "to do." Any movement one makes is called action or karma. One has done, one has been doing, one is doing, one will do, or one wants to do; all the actions done in the past, present, and future are called karmas. No one disputes the law of karma: "As you sow, so shall you reap." No religion in the world disputes this; neither do atheists. The law of action and reaction is accepted universally. Cause and effect, the twin laws of life, are inseparable, just like the two sides of a coin. One cannot escape from this inevitable law. No matter what happens, one has to follow it. There is no one who was ever born on this earth, no living creature, who has not followed this law. Karma is the universal law that cannot be avoided by anyone.

These karmas of past, present, and future can be described by the symbol of a bowman. The arrows a bowman has already sent toward the target are called past karmas, those arrows that he is holding in his hand to send are called present karmas, and those in the quiver on his back are called future karmas. One cannot do anything with past karmas unless he is fully enlightened. With knowledge of the Divine, the enlightened ones create the fire of knowledge that burns all the bondages created by past karmas. That is possible, but unless one has that ability, he has to reap the consequences of his past karmas. We cannot escape from that, but the present and future are in our hands.

Those who become aware of the law of karma do not miss this opportunity. They try to discipline themselves and direct their actions to the Divine only. The present shapes the future. They lead life from moment to moment, making it a beautiful poem and a joyous song. They enjoy life and create a new magnificent future for themselves by understanding the present life, rather than pondering over their past actions and brooding upon the deeds they have already performed. The force of the past definitely affects the present, but why should one waste the present in brooding on the past? Those who understand that what has happened in the past has happened, and decide to discipline themselves in the present, make the present glorious and create a better future. The past is past, and the greatest of all filters in life is called time. Casting your eyes toward past actions while living in the present is a misuse of time and energy. The past can never be recalled, though the memories of the past remain stored in the unconscious. We are still here and we can make our future. Everyone can make good use of the present and the future regardless of what has happened in the past.

Karma yoga focuses on those pages of the manuscript of life that one is holding in his hands, and that is the present. How does one study it? One can study it by knowing the law of karma. This is a very important thing to do. Awareness of one's karma, of one's actions in daily life, is essential. Two chapters of the manuscript of life are misplaced and lost, but the wise, by studying the present, easily establish a link to the missing pages of this manuscript. "Who am I? From where have I come? Why have I come? And where will I go?" These four questions compose a topic for research for all the students who are on the path, or who are inclined to choose a path for fulfilling the purpose of life. Every human being consciously or unconsciously is working toward perfection. All the paths lead to the same goal of perfection with the desire for liberation and happiness. These questions can be resolved by understanding the nature of the samskaras that motivate one to perform certain actions. Whatever we express through our mind, action, and speech has its roots in our motivations, mostly dormant, in the storehouse of our unconscious mind. It is a particular technique to study the unconscious and conscious mind and its interrelations. By studying the present actions, we can find out our past deeds and can also imagine our future.

Just as there are two aspects of life—life within and life outside—there are also two aspects of karma—karma performed mentally, and karma performed in the external world. The law is that if an individual acts, he will have to reap the fruits of his actions, so the kind of actions he does determines the result. If one sows the seed of an apple, he doesn't reap any other fruit; he can only reap an apple. Before one does any action outside, long before that, he has done some action within. The seed has been sown long before it becomes a tree that gives flowers and fruits. All things have their roots in the unknown, in the subtle world. The same law is applied to human beings. Anything that a human being does or wants to do, first he does within and then expresses it through action and speech. The seeds of all of one's actions, the motivations that move one to act, are the desires within him. Many hidden seeds of creative intelligence and seeds of disruptive motivations reside within us. Creative imagination and useless imagination, fancies, fantasies, symbols, and ideas all rise from the ocean of desire within. Desire motivates the thinking process, and one starts acting the way he desires. Then the fruits that he reaps from those deeds motivate him to do more and more deeds. One performs one's actions inside in a subtle way through his internal states long before they are expressed outside. Moving from one place to another does not change a person, because wherever he goes, he carries his internal states with him. And whatever is going on with him now will go on with him in the future if he does not control that which moves him—and that is the mind. If one does not think rightly, he cannot speak rightly; if one does not think rightly, he cannot act rightly. And if one does not do rightly, he can never reap the fruits of his desire from the tree of life. So one has to learn to think rightly, to keep one's internal states as tranquil as possible. Karma means that one has expressed a thought through his action or speech. But one should learn that one's speech and actions are virtually his thoughts.

A leaf being tossed by the wind and creating many patterns in the sky—is that leaf creating karma? And who is reaping the fruits of that karma? Is a human life controlled exactly like that wind-tossed leaf? No. A human being is alive and is far superior to that dead, lifeless leaf. Whenever one moves he is creating karma. But when one acts as if he is lifeless, then his environment creates the same situation for him—it controls his life. And when one acts like a human being, understanding his potentials, then he can act according to what he wants to accomplish. A human being does not act the way an animal acts. There is a difference, although the appetites equally influence both animals and human beings. As far as the appetites are concerned, a human being behaves exactly like an animal, but an animal is not considered to be like a human being. Human beings do the same things that animals do, but animals' activities are controlled by nature, while human beings' activities are not. Human beings are considered to be superior because they have free will to do what they want to do.

That is why all the great paths in the world talk about disciplining oneself. Self-discipline means guiding one's own mind, actions, and speech according to the desired goal: learning to understand what is not to be spoken and what is to be spoken, learning to understand what is not to be done and what is to be done. Otherwise one is a helpless slave of his inner whims. One has to learn to discipline himself so that his senses do not dissipate his energy and his mind. Once one has learned that, once he has control, his energies are at his disposal, and he can direct them according to his wish. Yet, even though people have intellect and free will, still they are captive, traveling in a narrow lane of action.

People cannot live without doing something; they have to do some actions. Someone might say he is not doing anything, but he is actually thinking, even if he is not aware of what he is thinking. People cannot live without doing some action, not even for a moment. And all of one's actions, whatever he performs from morning until evening—his useless actions, every word, every gesture—have some meaning. Why does one make certain gestures? Because of his inner thinking. All actions depend on the thinking process. The way one acts—that he is. So one can learn much about himself by studying his actions. One should ask oneself, "Why am I acting like this? I don't want to act this way, yet I am still doing it. Why?"

A vast portion of our thinking process is never materialized, for all that we think cannot be brought into actions because the instruments through which we perform our actions have limited capacity. A human being many times finds difficulty in expressing himself explicitly because of these limitations. Another helplessness is that he cannot remain without doing actions. And a further helplessness is that he has to reap the fruits of his actions, whether he wants to or not. The duties that he has chosen for himself bind him, and he does not know how to be free from them. There is great confusion regarding the performance of duties, even in the minds of great people who are considered to be the leaders of our society. This confusion exists because of a clash of interests. As is the case with two persons living together, so is the case with society. Our duties and commitments should be based on the interest of mutuality and not individuality, yet every individual does his duty for himself and not for the sake of others.

One's duties are very important; one cannot live without them. If those duties are not performed properly, one is unfulfilled and makes others unhappy. Duty is a commitment that we choose for ourselves, and action is a law of life and nature. Karma seems to be deeply mingled with both of these: action plus duty make karma. But even if one has learned how to do his duty, still he does not feel complete. He is fulfilling his commitment, but he is not trying to understand something deeper: one reaps the fruits of his actions, and they inspire him to do more actions. A couple buys a house—and immediately they need furniture, carpeting, and so on. They quickly find that one action immediately engages them in another action, and it becomes a chain reaction. They do not know how to deal with it, how to be free from this chain. They become so involved in it that they do not have time to think. There are many mysteries that are not unfolded because people get so involved in their so-called relationships in the world. One should learn to discharge his duties according to his or her ability and capacity, but should not let this keep one from the purpose of life. It is very interesting to study one's own self, but these days no one seems to have time because the objects of the world and so-called relationships have made people too busy.

When two people decide to get married, instead of learning to love each other and making sincere effort to attain the purpose of life, they keep each other busy for the fulfillment of their biological and psychological needs. They forget the purpose of married life and they create bondage for each other. When two people are involved with one another in this way, that is considered to be a great love in life. If a woman can keep a man busy for twenty-five years, he says, "My wife is wonderful!" But what did she do? She did not allow him to think for twenty-five years. And the husband did not allow her to think, either. When one has a child, he thinks the child is his primary concern, but he does not know what his real relationship with the child is. How did he choose this particular child, and how did the child choose his or her parents? There are many such questions to be answered, but one does not even attend fully to understanding the middle portion of the manuscript of life, because one is kept too busy by the actions and duties he has created for himself. People should not prevent their loved ones from contemplating on the vital questions of life. When two people meet and decide to join together, they can be helpful to each other. They should help each other in attaining the purpose of life, not postponing it. That could be a very fruitful relationship. One has to learn to understand oneself independently, and getting caught by the charms, temptations, and attractions of the world is not the way to do that.

Doing One's Duty with Love

People are caught in a state of confusion concerning the performance of their duty. Many times they don't want to do something, and yet they feel forced to do it. Whenever one does something in conflict it definitely gives a strain to the unconscious mind. Any action that one performs should not be done under pressure. Otherwise one might start developing and superimposing another nature on one's personality, and a time might come when the personality is completely changed. One should be spontaneous and honest when one relates to others.

Many people are doing their duty, yet they are unhappy, and the people for whom they are doing the duty are not satisfied either. These people are committing a serious mistake somewhere, because duty makes them slaves. One feels he is forced to do his duties even though he does not want to do them. If he doesn't do them, he suffers, and those who live around him also suffer. One cannot live without doing his duty, so one is helpless. He has to do his duty, and when he does his duty he becomes a slave. But the inborn desire for enlightenment again and again reminds him to accomplish the purpose of life. Changing one's situation—such as divorcing to attain a fake independence, or renouncing one's home and duties—will not solve this dilemma. One has to solve the main problem of how to have freedom from within and yet do one's duty. Because of this basic problem, one does not know how to enjoy life and live happily. People do their duty selfishly because of the pleasure they will receive. Even if one is doing something for his wife, his child, his brother, he is really doing it for himself, for what the others will do for him in return. Everyone is committing a mistake; no one knows how to do his duty with love.

What do we mean by love? Everyone says he loves his children and wife, but if he did, there would be no conflict. Conflict is a clear sign and symptom of a clouded mind that does not allow one to be in peace, and the mind which is not at peace does not help one to be happy. So that is not love. If one loves his duty, then he will enjoy doing it. But if one is unhappy, it is because he does not love selflessly; he has some expectation that is not being fulfilled. Love means being selfless. We have to live in a world where everybody forces things on us. This world is full of suggestions that blast us all the time—"Do this, do that." There is only one way to react, and that is to do one's duty lovingly. One should train oneself. "Why don't I like to do it?" A child does not like to read a book that has many difficult words. If his teacher forces a hard subject on him, the child will say, "That is useless information. I don't care if I don't find out." He does not like to know what he has not known; he wants to limit himself. He is afraid of facing the unknown and the difficult. We have formed that habit from our childhood. Every human being is afraid of the unknown and at the same time is not satisfied with the known. Being dissatisfied in the world and being afraid of the unknown makes one miserable. Both dissatisfaction and fear are the greatest enemies of mankind. Fear limits us. But there is no fear, no limitation in love. So one should learn to grease his duty with love. "I have to do it, and I like to do it." Then there will be no problem. One should learn to love his duty because one cannot live without doing it. It should be done for its own sake, because it is a must. That's very important.

All these conflicts in modern society that have given birth to so many psychological problems and so much sickness are a result of one great conflict: "I have to do it, but I don't want to do it, and I am forced to do it." Then people feel resentful and guilty, and they condemn themselves. They relate to only one thing: what is right and what is not right. So they become victims; they become sick. "I have not done anything right, but I have done many wrongs; I am a bad person." All the time they think of negative things. Negativity has become a part of their lives. It is not easy to come out of this. Every human being has weaknesses, but if one is constantly recognizing his weaknesses and not doing anything about them, he will become the victim of an incurable disease. No psychologist, no psychiatrist, no doctor, no yogi, no swami, no priest can help him. People are suffering more from self-created problems, miseries, and diseases than from the diseases that affect them arising from the external world. Why are people disturbed internally when no one has disturbed them? Why are they so depressed and gloomy? Because of their own thinking. Such negative thinking is selfish, fruitless, and injurious. It is better for one to think properly and to learn to love his duty; then there will be no problem. Creating love for one's duty will give freedom from stress.

Actually, modern man goes through stress and strain not because of the actions he performs but because of his attitude toward his whole life. Most people do not want to do their duties, yet they continue doing them. This brings a serious conflict between thinking and acting. This constant fight creates a battle within, which actually is the very cause of stress. In today's world, everyone seems to do things in reaction without thinking of the consequences of one's deeds and actions.

Duties Toward Oneself and Toward Others

There are two sets of duties that human beings perform in daily life: personal duties and duties toward others. By doing one's own ablutions, one is not obliging anyone; he is doing duty toward himself. Nature pushes one to perform one's personal duties—he must do them. When one goes to the bathroom, he is not obliging his neighbors—but if he doesn't, he will be disturbing his neighbors, because he'll become sick and consume the time of the people who have to attend him. If one is not doing his individual duty, then he is disturbing those who live with him. But even if one is doing his duty, he is taking care of himself only and is not serving others.

There is another set of duties that people perform; these

are the duties that they perform in relation to others every day. A person may feel, "I am not strong enough, but it is my duty to do this for him." Where does that sense come from? Not from the Lord; not from Jesus, or Moses, or Buddha, or Krishna. Our sense of duty has come from one thing: the natural law of karma. Why are we being active? Why are our legs and hands active? For the mouth. We do actions to learn something so we can eat. And why is the mouth active? For the liver. Why is the liver active? For the other parts of the body. Why are the other parts of the body active? For the whole being. Now if the mouth says, "OK, I want to be selfish, I don't want to give to the liver," what will happen to that person? His whole being will cease to exist. So is the case in a family, in society, and in a nation. This is a cosmic law. The natural law is that we are working for something higher than ourselves. The hands and feet are working for the mouth, the mouth is working for the liver, the liver is working for the other parts, and all the other parts are working for the whole being.

Karma yoga is the path of the person who is active in the world, the person with a family, with a job. He has to know how to communicate and how to relate well with others. In the external world, every action is related to somebody. Life in the external world means relationship. So first one has to learn to deal with this part of life that is called relationship; one has to learn how to relate with others. It is a great art. No psychology has yet perfected it because every human being is different, his thinking is different, his motivations are different. One has to interact, but some people develop a tendency of withdrawing. They become observers and constantly watch and evaluate what others are doing. They can become very good referees and judges in this way, but when we watch such people's own actions, we will find that their actions are worse than those of others. They neither observe themselves nor interact and get the reactions of others, so they cannot improve. Other people act, but without observing themselves. They also lose the effect of observation.

If he wants to relate to others properly, one should first understand the word *karma*. What does karma mean? In this context, it means more than just any action that someone performs. It means that action which does not create obstacles for others. Here karma is applied toward one's duties, one's own creations. Life is relationship, and, in a relationship, purposeful communication is one's duty. So one should learn to observe and listen to others and to observe and express oneself. Thus, one pleasantly performs his duty to communicate with others and to function better in the world.

The Things of the World Belong to No One

But there is another problem that one does not know how to deal with even if he has learned to do his duty lovingly. Every action brings a reaction, and one reaps the fruits of his actions. How can he get rid of those fruits and attain freedom from this endless cycle? What is that formula that one can practice in daily life? The great people of the world have tried to understand this law of karma, and there is one formula that they found, not through books, not through imagination, not through mere thinking, but through their own direct experience. That great idea is, "O man, all the things of the world are meant for you to use, but they are not yours. You can use them, but you have no right to claim proprietorship over them." This way all the objects of the world that obstruct human beings in attaining their goal become means. We do not train our children to understand this formula, and we were not trained in that direction either. That education is not imparted in childhood, so we develop a bad habit from the very beginning. We tell our children, "This is yours, this is yours." We don't teach them, "This is meant for you to use; enjoy it." So the children become victims of that false pride and think, "All things are mine"—but they are not. The things of the world belong to no one; everything here is constantly changing. Getting attached to the things of the world is very foolish. We should learn to understand this formula: "All the things of the world are meant for us. We should enjoy them and use them as means, but we cannot own them; we should not own them; they are not ours." This is very important. If one lives by this philosophy, one will be free. But, for this freedom, one needs to have inner strength. Constant awareness of the continuously changing patterns of the external world helps one to establish an attitude of nonattachment toward the temporal, and remembering the center of Consciousness that is eternal gives enormous strength in life. In the path of karma yoga, it is important to have this dual role to live happily and to go through this procession of life without any disturbance. Strength within always comes from constant awareness of the center of love or consciousness. The seeds of education should be sown in the hearts and minds of humans in early childhood: a tender bamboo shoot can be bent easily, but a mature plant cannot. It becomes very difficult—and in many cases, impossible—for one to change his thinking process in old age. That is why old age is considered to be full of follies.

The upbringing of a child seems to be the basic educational ground, for childhood habits are deep-rooted. Unfortunately, in modern times physicians, psychologists, and educators provide excuses to parents to be egotistical and to isolate the child. So the child is left alone, and he does not receive the care he should. If we don't impart right knowledge to the child, how can we expect the child to do better in life than the poor parents did? When a child does not see his parent being selfless, how can he become selfless? Later on, he comes to yoga seminars, and we teach him, "Be selfless, be selfless," but all his samskaras and training are full of, "Be selfish, be selfish." How can he understand our teaching? The child is father to the man, and so the same basic problem that is created in the child will occur in society. We must learn how to be selfless in our actions and then teach that to our children if our society is to be changed. Parents should learn to sacrifice a few of their joys for their children; then we would have a better society. But social data show that the most ignored class of our society is our children. Children are neglected—and yet every parent wants his children to be prosperous and grow as better human beings.

The Wise Surrender the Fruits

Doing all of one's actions for others—that is the way to liberation. The great people of the world have tried to go with the law of karma by doing their actions skillfully, selflessly, and lovingly, and by surrendering the fruits of their actions to others so that the fruits would not create bondage for them. But ordinary people do not do that. They get attached to the fruits and create a whirlpool for themselves.

The whirlpool of karma, which is created by our own ignorance, wants to annihilate our inborn desire for freedom, and many in this world are swept away by the glittering nature of the objects of the world. The Upanishads say, "*Tene tyaktena bhunjitha*"—"Therefore enjoy the objects of the world with renunciation." That is the difference between the ordinary person and the great person. Great is he who does all deeds selflessly for others. Petty and ignorant is he who does deeds for himself and gets attached and creates a whirlpool of misery for himself. When one applies the formula: "All the things of the world are for me, and I should learn to enjoy them and to use them, but they do not belong to me," then doing one's duty will not become an obstacle in the path of liberation. In such a case, the objects of the world do not create obstacles; they become means.

Here one has to understand the difference between what is pleasant and what is good. Today, someone sees some very pleasant thing and runs toward it, but tomorrow he finds that it is not pleasant anymore. What is pleasant now can be harmful the next moment. All the mistakes in the world are committed by people because of this: people know that something is pleasant but not good, and yet they do it. Nobody is ignorant. There are very few sins committed in innocence and ignorance. Crimes are committed knowingly because one is under the grip of the charms and temptations of the world, and so forms the habit. When the habit becomes deep-rooted, one becomes helpless, and performs harmful actions even though he knows that they are not proper. If one makes experiments, he'll find that good is different from pleasant. If he analyzes further he will find something more precious: the good alone is truly pleasant, because it leads one toward the desired goal. It is very difficult to come to that understanding. That is an advanced lesson. To realize it, one needs practice.

Practice means making constant sincere efforts. When a child is learning to walk, sometimes it stands, and sometimes it stumbles and falls. Many times the child falls, but that does not mean that the child should give up. In spiritual practice, people feel they are making progress one day, and the next day they feel they are going backward. But practice itself gives hope and strength. So one should practice understanding what is pleasant and what is good without focusing on his past mistakes.

Realizing Inner Strength and Perfection

It does not help to involve sin and God in all this. "Oh, I have committed mistakes; I am a sinner. There is no way for me; God alone can deliver me. God should do it." It is the result of one's own actions that he must reap, and only one's own actions in the present can free him. So one should be strong from within. Inner strength is the most helpful. External strength inspires one, but inner strength is the key point.

One can get rid of the bondage that he has been creating; he can get freedom from that whirlpool by skillfully, selflessly, and lovingly doing his actions and then surrendering the fruits of those actions to others. One does not have to abandon his actions and duties; he has to surrender the fruits of his actions. Every human being wants to improve, to unfold; he wants to attain freedom, to be eternally happy. This is every individual's desire, and to attain it, one must learn to do his actions skillfully. Next, one has to be selfless. If one is not selfless, he cannot go further. If one is selfish, then he says, "Everything is for me." If one is swimming in the ocean, and he tries to swim by drawing the water toward him, he will see the effect of such an attitude—he will discover that this is not the way to swim; this is the way to drown. It is not the way of going to the other shore. All the selfish people in the world are continually drowning themselves and creating miseries for others because they do not know any better. But if they are taught properly, if they are made aware that selfishness is not healthy but injurious, then they will understand and learn how to cross the ocean of delusion.

In the Sermon on the Mount, Jesus taught that we are perfect like our Father but that we need growth. All people have the potential for perfection, but because of inertia, irresponsibility, selfishness, and lack of training, they remain incomplete. The Bhagavad Gita also repeats, "*Aksaram brahma paramam.* . . .—the highest imperishable principle is Brahman. Its existence as the embodied soul is called *Adhyatma.*" If a human being does not understand that center within which is limitless, then he is caught with thinking that he is limited; he is in bondage, he is suffering. But when he examines all the levels of life, he will come to understand that limitation is self-imposed by his own thinking and that misery and pain can be transcended. One thing is very important in helping to realize one's perfection: to be nonattached. One should do his best in a skillful and selfless way, and he should not claim ownership over the fruits of his actions or the objects of the world. This is a very simple formula to be practiced.

Marriage should also be based on these principles. When people expect too much from marriage, then they are bound to become disappointed. One enters into a marriage relationship because he feels insecure, and he thinks he will be safe. But insecurity comes out of fear and ignorance, and it continues; marriage does not solve this problem. People remain insecure, fearing that their husband or wife will stop loving them or that they might desert them. Older people become insecure because they know that one day their spouse will die, and nobody will be their companion or take care of them. One should be bold enough to be prepared for all the eventualities of life. Two people create a relationship, but through it they find pain and misery for themselves by being insecure and attached—and then they pray to God for peace and happiness. How is God going to help them when they are constantly creating problems for themselves? Such a prayer is not fruitful at all. Suppose one prays, "O Lord, I don't want to chew my food. Will you please help me to digest it?" It's never going to happen. One should learn to understand where prayer should be applied and where not. Each person has a level of awareness on which he understands his responsibility, where he knows that he is competent to find out, to seek for himself and to attain. One should learn the right way to seek that wisdom that gives freedom from pain, misery, and ignorance.

People think that marriage is a solution to all of life's questions, but that is not true. Marriage provides a companionship in which two people understand each other; it is a partnership in which they help each other to try to attain the ultimate goal. Many people also think that if a person loves somebody, he should be able to fight with the one he loves. Wives often say that fighting is very healthy and that it is actually a part of modern therapy. What a bankruptcy of the modern mind and culture, that fighting is a therapy! One should be proud of one's spouse, one should be proud of one's children, and one should have self-pride. One should learn to appreciate one's family and to appreciate oneself. But there is no couple who have not thought at times that they have been caught by marriage. Socially and personally, they have been paying attention and doing all their duties nicely, but all the time they feel they are caught. How does one get rid of such a feeling? One feels like a slave because he does not know the proper way to do his duties. It's a matter of attitude. If one learns to do his duty lovingly, it will not be a burden, it will not create a problem for him.

Love Means Giving

Before one learns to love someone, one should learn to understand and accept that person as he or she is. This acceptance does not mean forgiving the other for his or her mistakes. Unconditional acceptance is the main prerequisite and primary step for learning to love someone. Many people say that love dies. I do not believe that love ever dies; if something dies or changes, it was never love. Actually, learning to love is real learning, and all other branches of learning are meant to support this. When we say love is divine, this is a phrase we use without understanding it. Love is an understanding that continues to learn and move upward, and finally reaches the ultimate heights, the love of Love. Karma is an expression of that love which we learn through understanding all our duties. If all our duties are performed with love, this will create heaven on earth. Heaven is another idea created by selfish people, and hell is an idea created by weak people. These two ideas were used for exploitation by certain clever people. What chaos! When a human being learns to love his duty, faithfully and sincerely as much as he understands, he is in love and such a love leads him to happiness.

Love and duty are a creation of the human mind and heart. All other things of the world are created by Providence and manifested by the ultimate Reality. No human being can create anything; a person can only join one thing to another. He can unite two things together, and this unity is his urge to love. So love and karma, if properly learned and performed, can establish a living heaven on earth.

One's actions can be the expression of his love. What is that love with which one should perform his duties? Love means giving. Giving is the highest of all actions in the world, and giving alone can bestow freedom. If one does not learn to give, he can never attain freedom. Even if one is doing the best of actions, the greatest and most wonderful karmas, if he is reaping the fruits for his own self, then those fruits are motivating him, and his attachment will create more and more bondage for him. That is not freedom. We cannot stop doing karma, but we can stop being in the bondage of karma because it is not karma that binds us, but the fruits received therefrom. So if we offer the fruits of our actions to others, we will be free from the bondage created by our karma. If all human beings would keep only as much as they need—not as much as they want—our whole society would be happy.

A rich person learns to give to others not because he wants to give, but because he finds that giving is a necessity of life. If someone has everything, he does not know what to do with his wealth; it becomes a great burden. Everyone wants to become rich—but any rich person will say, "You don't know what a burden I have." The burden is not in having money; it is in having a sense of ownership. So a rich person learns to give because he wants to get rid of that burden. People do charity for three reasons: some for name and fame, others thinking that it is a good deed and that they will receive in abundance in the next life, and a few give selflessly. The third act seems to be more rational and philosophical. When one gets attached to his possessions, then nature one day whispers the secret of giving just to release him from his false and egotistical possessiveness. To be released from this bondage is one of the virtues we should learn in our daily life. The best of charity relieves us from the bondage of attachment we have created for our wealth, home, and other possessions. The renunciates renounce them and go away. If they still remember them and feel attachment to the possessions, their renunciation becomes fake. Such a renunciation creates agony in the human mind. But one can live in the world doing his duty and offering the fruits of his actions for others. The path of renunciation and the path of selfless action each rewards in the same way. The renunciate is not superior to the person who lives in the world and serves others selflessly. After analyzing the fleeting nature of the objects of the world and the way self-created misery is imposed on oneself, the wise man learns to do his actions and give away the fruits to others. This is a constant prayer and a real worship, according to the path of karma yoga.

The Cycle of Reincarnation

Every person has come to this plane to attain perfection and be free from the burden of confusion that he has created for himself in the past. But because of deep-rooted habits, he creates problems for himself instead. Has he come to create more problems for himself? No. Then why is he doing it? The answer is that he has bad habits. People become victims of their habits, and yet they are the creators of those habits. They create their own circumstances. The circumstances do not create the people, and yet the people blame their circumstances, their relationships, their associates. This happens because they are in deep ignorance. They do not understand that their unhappiness is not created by others but by their own actions and thinking.

It is a serious mistake to think that individuals live only

once. It is also a mistake to say that God, the Almighty or the Creator of this universe, has created the individuals as they are. The law of equality, love, and justice cannot possibly be unjust and cruel to one and make others happy. Actually, the individual soul is incarnated many times, according to one's own karma. But the philosophy of reincarnation is a strange concept to Western religions and traditions, and is seldom discussed. Nonetheless several Western philosophers—among them, Plato, Schopenhauer, and Hegel—have believed in reincarnation. Plato believed that knowledge was built up in this life on the foundation of learning and experiences gained in previous lives. The philosophy of karma leads to the conclusion that nothing happens by accident. The philosophy of karma does not, however, believe in fatalistic ideas. Whatever happens is the result of previous choices, actions, and samskaras. What happens to us now is the fulfillment of what we have done in the past, and what is to be in the future will likewise be the result of present actions.

In the eternal cycle of human evolution, one gets status and power to choose, determine, and decide what he wants to do. The advantage of reincarnation is to provide a human being with enough opportunities so that he can fulfill the purpose of life. Is it possible for one to attain perfection in one lifetime? Why have human beings been created, and who created them? Is the Creator just, having created such a miserable world? When such questions arise in his mind, the religionist cannot furnish logical answers. But the philosophy of karma explains that it is one's karma, one's actions, one's deeds that are responsible for his present condition. A human being has free will to create his own destiny; he can attain the purpose of his life and overcome the bondage created by his past karmas. The moment one comes to this realization, he starts practicing, and changes his habits. A selfish person can learn to give if he knows that giving, serving, and offering the fruits of his actions will bring liberation to him.

Unity in Diversity

At first people give, not because they love others, but because giving gives them freedom. This is the first step of love, when one becomes aware that it is not healthy for him to hold, but that he should give. Why does anyone want to do something for others? Where does this motivation come from? When someone sits down at the dinner table, no matter how great a friend he has sitting beside him, he won't put his food into his friend's mouth. Automatically, his hand goes to his own mouth. So where does this loving tendency in human beings come from? That love comes when one has become aware of the unity in diversity and realizes that we are all essentially one.

When does one test his love for others, when does he examine it? Suppose a house is in flames and there is a child inside. The family and neighbors are cowards and do nothing, but suddenly a stranger comes and jumps in that flaming house to rescue the child. He has no association with the child, but he identifies with the child's life. He protects that child because he feels no boundary between his essence and the child's essence. Most people think that if someone loves his spouse and children, that at the same time he must exclude others who are not close to him. But this is not right; this is not called love. True love is universal; it is not limited to a select few but is extended to all.

Three Universal Qualities

If people would learn to understand and to practice three principles, they could learn how to love others. Everyone can learn how to love others; love is a very practical, down-to-earth philosophy that anyone can practice. For learning how to love in one's family life and in the world, the first principle one should understand is not to snatch anyone else's rights. Everyone has his own rights. So, first of all, one should not rob the rights of the people with whom he lives. Next, one should learn to give up his own rights for others. The best way to live in a society, in a community, in a family is this: give up your own rights for others and don't deprive others of their rights. With this principle, anyone can learn to love. The third principle is honesty and sincerity in one's relationships. How can someone really love another person and at the same time cheat that person, be dishonest, or be insincere with the person whom he says he loves? It's not possible. To love and to be dishonest are two different expressions.

If any individual really wants to be free, he will have to improve himself in three dimensions: giving freely, loving freely, and being selfless. One can very easily live happily in life provided he understands these three things: learn to give, learn to love, learn to be selfless. These are universal qualities, and by learning these, an individual can unfold himself so that he becomes universal. That is called progress. One can watch his progress by observing to what extent he has developed these qualities. If one does not find these qualities in himself, if one is being petty, if he is not expanding his consciousness, then he is not progressing.

People are born, and they are sure to die. One doesn't know how long he will stay on this platform. He has come as a guest on a voyage, on a training program, but here he establishes his ownership. He makes many, many arrangements; he tries his best to soothe his senses, to stimulate his mind, and to be comfortable. But the aging process troubles him and death opposes him, and then he cries. Finally nature gives him a harsh shock and says, "You are no longer fit for my theatre. Get out of this park!" A time comes when everyone wonders what will happen to him when he dies. Almost everyone is afraid to leave this platform, and yet nobody is satisfied in this world, no one is happy. People continue to fight to remain here, when they know that no one has ever attained happiness here. People do not want to leave this platform because they have developed many, many attachments, and they have not developed self-awareness or awareness for the truth. They know that the body is subject to change, death, and decay, but they ignore this fact, and everyone fights against leaving this platform. Even medical science today helps people in fighting during that time when actually one needs peace of mind. Religious ministers and priests often describe how great and glorious the next world is—but they don't find delight in dying, with anticipation of enjoying the next world's pleasures.

Those who are not liberated here cannot be liberated in the next world; that they can be is just a myth. I am not liberated in this room, but I think that by going to another room I will be liberated. Who is going to liberate me there? I am in bondage now, because I have put myself into this situation. I created this bondage for myself, but I expect God to release me from that bondage in the next room. God is not responsible for my bondage, and so he is not responsible for my release either. Each person creates his own bondage, and he has to release himself. People have to learn to be happy here. But instead they create many, many desires for themselves, and when they cannot fulfill those desires, they get frustrated. What an impossible way to create happiness for oneself! One should look within and try to examine the deeper levels of his being, where all his desires and motivations reside.

Training Oneself to be Happy in Mind, Action, and Speech

Freedom is possible if one learns to discipline himself on three levels: mind, action, and speech. First, one should train the mind in a positive way and not be negative. People waste so much time in negative thoughts, expressions, actions, and talk. That is not at all productive. One should learn to develop a sense of humor. If one doesn't have that, then he is really missing something. One can have all the amenities of life and very refined tastes and aesthetic sense, but if he has not developed a sense of humor within himself, he is depriving himself. Such a man remains lonely. Even during trying circumstances, humor can be maintained. Humor is a great friend indeed.

There is a story about the humor of Socrates, who is considered to be the father of Western philosophy. One day he was philosophizing and his wife wanted to talk to him. She was a very nagging woman, and I don't blame her, because she was married to a philosopher who wouldn't cater to her whims. She wanted attention, and Socrates was busy philosophizing, so she brought a bucketful of water and poured it over him. Socrates just looked at his students and said, "I always heard that thundering clouds do not rain, but that's not true!" He did not lose his temper; he did not react to the negative side of his wife. That's how they could live together. But what happens with most people? If someone becomes emotional, the other person completely loses his cheerfulness and becomes even more emotional. This is one of the problems that creates bad relationships in the world. People react negatively to the negativity of others, and it never stops. Modern man does not know how to smile. He has to slap his cheeks and then smile, and then force a laugh because real laughter does not come from within him. Negative thinking destroys humor; but positive thinking cultivates positive reactions and creates humor and joy. One should learn to be positive all the time.

What is the sign of positivity? Action. A thought loses its value unless it is allowed to be expressed through action or speech. All action is initially a thought. Before one allows a thought to come into action, one should examine it. One should ask himself, "Am I doing right? Is it beneficial for others?" The highest thought is that which is completely beneficial for others, where one is not personally involved. Positivity means that a positive thought wants to materialize itself into action, and one decides, "I will do it; I can do it; I am going to do it." When one gradually builds this determination and acts accordingly, then he gets the strength of self-determination. If one is positive in self-determination, then one has attained a great deal.

The gist of all the bibles in the world is to have right thought, right action, and right speech—to have control of mind, action, and speech. Fundamentally, the spiritual truths behind all the religions of the world are one and the same. There is no basic difference, although they vary according to the times, the culture, the location, and the climate. Custom, ritual, and system change according to the environment of a country, and in all religions these become dominant, so that the ultimate truth is obscured. One has certain duties toward his family, his society, his country, and, finally, to the whole of humanity. At the same time, one has a duty of enlightening oneself. Everyone should learn to adjust, fulfilling all of these duties by living in the world and remaining above.

One should understand not to disturb others and not to disturb oneself. If one is disturbed and says, "So what if I am depressed; so what if I am sick? I am not disturbing anyone. Why are people worried?" then he is wrong. When one is disturbed, he gives "bad vibes" to others. If a jar of cold water is placed next to a jar of hot water, the cold water will start getting warm. That's called the law of association, and we all are affected by that law. If I find someone in great agony, I will feel sad. People don't cry only because they are in pain; often they cry because others are crying. The law of association and identification affects people and makes them forget their essential nature. But one can learn to remain unaffected by the negativity of others. One should learn the art of living so his equilibrium remains undisturbed and, thus, he can remain unaffected by adverse circumstances. Then, by doing those positive actions that are helpful to oneself and not harmful for others, one will have self-confidence and inner strength, and one needs inner strength to enlighten himself and remain happy in the world. Almost all actions are enveloped by the appetites of food, sex, sleep, and self-preservation, but any action that is free from these is a selfless action, and that is very helpful. One should learn to use the law of action to perform those actions that are not unhealthy for oneself and for others.

The duties that one performs in daily life are very important, for without doing one's duty, one cannot survive. But even when one does his duty with his full ability, he will find that the duty has made him a slave unless he does it with nonattachment. The path of karma claims to be able to give freedom, and it says that one can attain that liberation here, whether one believes in God or not. People are doing their actions because they cannot live without doing actions. One has to do something, and when one does something, he reaps something, and that something motivates him to do something more. That's how one creates the whirlpool. But there is an escape from that chain, there is a proper way of doing things. If one goes on doing his duties but gives the fruits of his actions to others willingly, then he is free. That which binds one is the fruit of his actions, but one who does his karma for the sake of others becomes a great one—like the sun, for example. Has anyone ever seen the sun shouting, "O creatures, I am giving you light and life! Will you adore me and praise me?" The sun has never done that. The greatest of all examples is the sun—it shines selflessly for all. There is no darkness under the sun. Yet the sun remains above and far away. One has to learn to live in the world exactly like the sun, who shines for all and shines for himself and yet remains above. That is called living in the world yet remaining above.

In the path of karma, one should aspire to live for at least a hundred years, but only to perform his actions, his duties. One who aspires to live for a long time just to enjoy pleasures without doing his duties creates the bondage of attachment. Even the wise often get confused and cannot decide what is right and what is not. But if someone practices by performing his duties selflessly, skillfully, and lovingly, and he commits a mistake, he soon rectifies his mistake by the quest of truth. In the philosophy of karma yoga, actions are not renounced, but the fruits of the actions are renounced for the sake of others. Therefore, one should go on doing his duties for the sake of others until the last breath of his life.

Karma without love is bondage. Karma with love is freedom. Liberation from the bondage of karma is attained the way it has been explained in the eighteenth chapter of the Bhagavad Gita: "O Arjuna, renounce all thy duties and take refuge in me alone. I will liberate you from all the sins." When one learns to do his duties for his family members and then learns to do his duty for his neighbors, then for his nation, and in the end, for humanity, he no longer creates bondage for himself.

Chapter 5

Raja Yoga

The Path of Discipline and Meditation

Raja yoga, the royal path, is a very scientific and systematic path that suits modern man. It is a very practical path that was systematized and codified thousands of years ago by the sage Patanjali. By following this path, one learns to control and direct all his energy, desires, emotions, and thoughts to the center of consciousness and attain samadhi. The purpose of this path is to lead one to the state of samadhi in which the individual unites himself with the cosmic Reality. There are eight rungs in the ladder of raja yoga that are systematically attained until the aspirant finally achieves his goal. Practicing raja yoga is like climbing on a ladder. If the student steps on one rung, then he becomes aware of the next rung. The goal of this path is to unite the individual soul with the cosmic Soul, and this union is called samadhi. This is a state in which one resolves all his questions because he has attained oneness with the ultimate Reality. One who has attained samadhi attains a state of perfection.

Raja yoga encompasses teachings from the other paths of yoga; they are not mutually exclusive. Raja yoga includes various methods within one system, and it can be practiced by people of varying backgrounds and temperaments. It imparts a practical training program within three realms: physical, mental, and spiritual. Through its practicality one achieves mastery and thus attains full realization of the Self. It is a systematic discipline that does not believe in imposing an unquestioning faith on anyone, but always encourages and strengthens a healthy faculty of discrimination. In this path, certain methods are prescribed along with explanations of their benefits so that the raja yoga methods can be scientifically verified time after time. The students of this path accept its methods as hypotheses to be tested by their own experience. For this reason, raja yoga is suited to modern students, for whom skepticism is almost a religion.

This path is actually called *astanga yoga*—the yoga of eight limbs. It is called raja yoga because of its magnificent and majestic way of practice. On all other paths there are vague instructions, philosphical expositions, few practical methods, and no way of examining one's own progress. But in this path, the student can examine his own progress. Here, philosophy and practice are inseparably mingled. Other systems say, "Do this, and do not do that." But this system teaches one how to be. Direct experience is the very leader on this path.

A solid philosophy, called Samkhya philosophy, stands behind this science. This is the most ancient philosophy of the world. *Samyak akhyate* means "that which explains the whole in its entirety." The philosophy of Samkhya is the mother of all sciences. It gave birth to mathematics, and all the branches of science are based on and depend on mathematics. The Bhagavad Gita says that the learned do not differentiate or separate Samkhya and yoga science—*"Samkhya yoga prathak. . . ."* This philosophy is considered by logicians to be down-to-earth and practical. It acknowledges that human beings are in pain and misery. It also recognizes that there is a cause for misery and that there is a way of having freedom from misery. And finally, it says that a state can be attained, which is a state of freedom. For attaining freedom and samadhi, yoga science furnishes many methods within one definite system.

Yoga is the exact science that helps one to know one's own internal states. The application of this science traces its path of revelation and control from the gross (the physical body), to the more subtle (the senses), to the subtlemost manifestations of the mind, and then to the center of consciousness—the individual soul. This yogic discipline is an eightfold path. These eight steps are *yama, niyama, asana, pranayama, pratyahara, dharana, dhyana,* and *samadhi.*

The first four steps—yama, niyama, asana, and prana-yama—comprise the path of hatha yoga, which is auxiliary and preliminary to the other four steps of raja yoga. The yamas and niyamas, the ten commitments of yoga science, are the first two rungs on the ladder of raja yoga. The five yamas are: non-violence, truthfulness, non-stealing, continence, and non-possessiveness. The practice of these restraints leads the student to behavioral modifications in which all weaknesses and imperfections are replaced by positive virtues. The five niyamas are: cleanliness, contentment, practices that bring about perfection, study of the scriptures, and surrender to God. The niyamas help one to regulate and modify one's habit patterns and lead one to the control of one's behavior. Thus one can transform one's personality with less effort in a short time.

Beginners should not ignore the importance of these first two steps of the yoga ladder. If someone practices the yamas and niyamas with mind, action, and speech, he can attain enlightenment. With constant and persistant effort, the student will eventually be able to practice them as conscientiously as he can. Yoga teachers in the West teach the yoga exercises along with certain breathing exercises, but the yamas and niyamas are neglected because of the difficulty the students would have and the changes of life style that are necessary in order to practice them. Actually, hatha yoga as a complete system has degenerated into a cult of physical beauty and prolonged youth. Asanas and pranayama do insure physical health, beauty, and coordination, it's true, but the full benefits of hatha yoga science are not generally realized. The full benefits can be realized by the students only when their minds are free from violent, distracting, and dissipating thoughts and emotions. It is the practice of the yamas and niyamas that enables students to cultivate steady and tranquil minds.

The mind and body interact to a greater extent than is normally understood. In fact, scientific experiments indicate that most diseases are physical manifestations of thinking and emotional disturbances. Physical health is mainly dependent on mental health. It therefore becomes important to cultivate mental attitudes that insure a steady and tranquil mind—mental health—before one turns his attention to physical health. That is why in this system asana and pranayama, the third and fourth rungs of the yoga ladder, are preceded by the yamas and niyamas. If the mind is constantly subject to disturbing emotions and thoughts, the resulting bodily disturbances cannot be combated by practicing postures alone. The practice of asanas and pranayama is therefore very limited if they are not taught in conjunction with the yamas and niyamas, the ten commitments of the science of raja yoga.

The Yamas

Human life has two aspects: internal and external. One helps the human being to relate to others, and the other helps him to know himself on all levels. The yamas, or restraints, are a way of practicing the art of living in the external world. If these five observances are practiced in daily life, the flower of humanity will bloom and there will be happiness everywhere.

Ahimsa means non-injuring, non-hurting, and non-killing. Normally, students think of violence only in physical terms, and civilized people refrain from gross acts of violence because of legal and social pressures. But ahimsa refers to non-violence in thought, action, and speech. All actions and speech are directed by the mind. Therefore, violence in speech or action is always preceded by violent thoughts. This has serious repercussions on the mental life and also reflections on the body. Practicing ahimsa shows one how to avoid these consciously and to be aware of the fact that violence is injurious to the mind and body, as well as to those toward whom one expresses violence. The practice of ahimsa leads one toward the service of others, for its careful cultivation leads to a spontaneous and all-encompassing love. Ahimsa is a very practical way of expressing one's love toward others. By not injuring, harming, hurting, and killing, one is learning to practice to love others, and loving others is the highest of all worships.

Correctly practicing truthfulness is impossible without practicing ahimsa. To be truthful and to speak truth become necessary for students if they really want to know their essential nature, but the students find difficulty in practicing truth because they do not know how. It is necessary to not lie, and by not lying, one learns to speak truth. By not performing violent actions and not having violent thoughts, one can practice and express his love. Only the strong can practice ahimsa. Violence and weakness are synonymous. Ahimsa, being an expression of love, brings strength and confidence within. Self-confidence comes only when ahimsa is practiced.

Here the student should note that truthfulness is the second commitment and ahimsa is the first, which indicates that practicing truthfulness is essential, but ahimsa, being an expression of love, is practiced first. In all the disciplines of all traditions, truthfulness is considered to be the highest of all courts, but how does one practice it? One should be truthful to

oneself first. By not being truthful, one creates a dual personality, which weakens human potential and robs inner strength.
When the student learns not to lie, he realizes that one lie
inevitably leads to another, and soon deception becomes second
nature and leads to a fearful and scheming mind. It is a fact that
when a student makes truth the central focus of his life, all his
utterances are effective and come true. Such a student never lies.
Practicing truthfulness is a way of storing inner strength, and
once one builds a strong reservoir of strength within, he can
attain the higher steps of realization. Those who are the students
of truth realize that truth is the lord of their life. Such students
are fearless and do not suffer on account of complexes.

Asteya means non-stealing, which means to completely
shun the desire to take other people's possessions in their absence
and without their permission. Non-stealing includes refraining
from misappropriation, accepting bribes, and the like. The
desire for what others own can be very tempting, and it charms
the ordinary mind all the time. It creates guilt feelings and
weakens the inner frame of life. The stealing habit is devious, and
it creates a sense of inadequacy and jealousy. Such a person
always remains unsatisfied, frustrated, and unfulfilled because he
depends on the objects others own. The thought of stealing never
gives comfort to anyone. Non-stealing gives self-confidence,
adequacy, and peace of mind. Cultivating non-stealing helps one
develop a sense of fulfillment and completeness. It leads one to
the state of freedom from cravings. Those who understand their
inner states of mind, know that human progress is not possible
without practicing asteya. The habit of stealing can create a deep
groove in the unconscious and finally lead one to become
a professional thief. When such people are interrogated, they
admit that stealing is their habit. For lack of training, people
pick up such habits, and if such people are not trained, no matter
how much punishment they receive, they will never be trans-

formed. Stealing is a symptom of great insecurity. One wants to have unauthorized occupation and ownership of others' possessions. This creates a great barrier in self-improvement. The students of yoga are made aware of these commitments so that they develop inner strength and other essential virtues which help them to rise above such habits. The human personality is woven by habits, and habits are created by repeated actions. One becomes helpless and thus becomes a victim of mental disorders.

Brahmacharya means to walk in the Brahman, the universal consciousness. Brahman is the fountainhead and source of life, light, and all energies, and the student who learns to have constant awareness directs all his energies toward knowing Brahman alone. One who cultivates this yama is constantly aware of Brahman, who is the source of life, light, and the existence of all. When one learns to direct his entire energy through word, deed, and thought toward Brahman alone, he is practicing Brahmacharya. Such a state of mind is possible only when it is free from sensuality and all sensual desires. Among all urges and motivations that play a great role in human life and actually control the creatures of the world, the sexual urge is one of the most powerful urges, and if not properly controlled and directed, it could be a destructive one. Brahmacharya, therefore, is often understood as abstinence from sex and is called celibacy. In reality, it refers to continence in either the celibate or the married states, for sexual excesses lead one to the dissipation and waste of vital energy which could instead be directed or channeled to attain the higher states of consciousness. Many ignorant people think that the repression and suppression of sexual energy is called Brahmacharya. But when one starts repressing and suppressing sexual desires, one's repressions lead to frustration and thus to an abnormal state of mind. When repression and suppression start controlling human life, one always remains mentally imbalanced and loses physical coordination. This can create many psychosomatic disorders. The person is angry, frustrated, depressed, conceited, starts overeating, and loses touch with reality. Such a self-centered person never makes himself or herself happy and can create disaster for himself and others. Actually, it is one of the greatest arts of living to direct this energy and channel it for higher use. Many in today's society, when they lose control of this appetite, become perverts and nymphomaniacs. This is a disease which is deep-rooted. Brahmacharya, in its first stage, means to have control over sensual cravings. The bliss, happiness, and peace that accompanies Self-realization is far greater than any transient pleasures, and one who is committed to the path of enlightenment would therefore overcome the obstacles of sensual cravings without any kind of repression or suppression.

Aparigraha means non-possessiveness or non-hoarding. This word is often misunderstood to mean self-denial, to be without any material possessions. By the practice of not desiring to possess more than one needs, one can foster an inward attitude rather than mere outward appearance. It is a time-consuming factor to accumulate, possess, and own things that are not used in our daily life. Actually it is an obsession and addiction to accumulate things that are not necessary. Such a tendency makes one a beggar. A beggar can be more attached to his begging bowl than a king to his crown. The danger lies both in having useless possessions and in becoming attached to them. There is no end for a person when he forms the habit of having material possessions. Modern society is oriented toward having possessions that are actually not needed and not helpful in any way, like having many houses, accumulating more wealth than is needed, and the like. The more one possesses, the more one becomes attached. It is attachment that creates misery. Aparigraha, if practiced properly and sincerely, leads one to peace of mind.

The Niyamas

Every human being has two aspects of life—within and without, internal and external. The yamas help one to live happily in the external world, and the five niyamas help one to develop self-awareness and self-control. These two sets of commitments prepare a student for samadhi, the highest state described in the path of raja yoga. The five niyamas or observances are helpful for understanding oneself on all dimensions. The niyamas are: *saucha,* cleanliness or purity; *samtosha,* contentment; *tapas,* the practices that lead to perfection of body, mind, and senses; *svadhyaya,* study of the self, the book of life, and sayings of the great sages, which leads the student to the knowledge of the ultimate Reality; and *Ishvara pranidhana,* surrendering oneself to the ultimate goal of life, the ultimate Truth. After faithfully following this course of conduct the student acquires serenity of mind and equilibrium.

Saucha means cleanliness and purity, both of the body and the mind. Purity of the body is easily practiced, but purity of the mind needs a sincere, honest, and constant effort. And once the purity of mind is attained, then one is fully prepared for the inner voyage. To achieve this state, one should cultivate constant awareness by being mindful all the time. To purify the buddhi, or the faculty of discrimination, is the most important task. When one remains always aware of one's thoughts and learns to discriminate between pure and impure thoughts, helpful and disturbing thoughts, he develops the sense of determination and strengthens his will and thus does not allow the seeds of impure thoughts to grow within. When the faculty of discrimination is sharpened and a student knows that impure thoughts lead to greater bondage and create obstacles, he then strengthens the pure thoughts. With all sincerity and perseverance one can cultivate saucha in thought, action, and speech.

Samtosa—contentment—is a state of mind that is not dependent on one's worldly status, material possessions, or the wealth he owns. For instance, a beggar can be as content as anyone. In fact, some of the renunciates are more content than the kings, presidents, and leaders of the world. Human desires are never fulfilled by worldly attainments, and if a desire is fulfilled, another arises. These desires constantly agitate and irritate the mind, and such a mind cannot be in peace and attain tranquility. But by cultivating samtosha one can remain in a state of tranquility and equilibrium in all circumstances. The word "contentment" should not be mistaken for sloth and should not lead the student to slackening off the efforts he is making for self-improvement and unfoldment. A discontented person remains passive, and life becomes dull. One who is content makes efforts with a sense of duty and serves others all the time. A person who is not content can never be a good server. A person should not be satisfied as far as his efforts for attaining his goal are concerned, but he should always remain content. If one has made full sincere efforts in attaining his goal, and he does not receive the fruits or success according to his estimation, even then he should learn to be content. It is human nature that people work for certain goals, and many times, even after making complete and sincere efforts, one may not accomplish his desired goal. Discontentment arises in such a state of mind. Contentment is a great virtue that one can cultivate in his daily life. When sincere efforts stem from a sense of duty and selfless service instead of from discontentment or anticipation of the fruits of one's efforts, contentment comes. It is one of the greatest of all wealths. Students often become disillusioned and disappointed if they do not experience the signs and symptoms of progress. Contentment is the greatest of all wealths that one can have. It gives freedom from anxiety and worries.

Tapas has often been misinterpreted as mortification of

the flesh and excessive austerity, as exemplified by hair shirts and beds of nails. This is torture and not at all tapas. In the Bhagavad Gita, the Lord clearly explains that yoga is not for those who are teased by the flesh, not for those who torture the flesh. Literally, tapas means that which generates the Divine fire. Heat arises within those who are full of spiritual fervor with the zeal of burning desire for attaining samadhi. Acts that increase this spiritual fervor constitute tapas; a simple life that is free from sensual indulgence, regulated fasting, remembering the Lord's name all the time, serving one's fellow man according to one's ability and capacity—all constitute tapas. Actually, the mind expresses itself through the senses. The five subtle senses (hearing, tasting, touching, smelling, and seeing) are the subtle avenues through which one perceives the world. The five gross senses (mouth, hands and feet, and the senses of elimination) are the avenues through which the mind expresses itself in the external world. If these senses are not trained and regulated, one cannot communicate properly with others. For proper communication with the help of tapas one learns to have command and control over one's expressions and sense perception so that the outgoing tendencies of the senses and sense perception are conducted in such a way that mind doesn't lose its orderliness. The senses do disturb the mind if they are not orderly, but with the help of tapas, the senses are trained to function properly. Tapas helps the mind to be undissipated and undistracted by external stimuli. Such a mind is capable of fathoming the deeper levels and does not become a source of distraction. Mortification of the flesh or torturing oneself has no value as far as tapas is concerned.

Svadhyaya is a study leading to the knowledge of Self-realization. This study is conducted on two dimensions and not simply by studying the sayings of the great sages, or the scriptures. The sayings of the great sages do inspire and support the student in the pursuit of his practices. But studying one's own thoughts, emotions, deeds, and actions is the real study. The scriptures and other books of spiritual value help the student, for many great sages and yogis who have trodden the path of enlightenment have imparted their direct experience, and such knowledge is very helpful, especially when the student faces certain obstacles on the path. Mere study of the scriptures is the sort of information that is really not knowledge, but only a part of knowing. We intellectually know many things, yet our ignorance is not dispelled. By self-study, or studying within and without, we experience directly that which dispels the darkness of avidya, or ignorance. The great sages, the yogis, impart their practical experience, and this rational acceptance of spiritual truths leads the student to the higher state, the source of intuition. The finest source of all knowledge opens itself and then the true understanding of life and its purpose is understood. Only when one has carefully learned the study of his own internal states will the true knowledge of the Self begin to dawn.

Ishvara pranidhana, surrender to the ultimate Truth or Reality, is possible only with immense faith and complete dedication. Total surrender is possible only when one constantly practices with full sincerity, faithfulness, and dedication. Ishvara is that center of consciousness within us that is the Lord of life, seated beyond body, senses, breath, and mind, deeply buried in the inner chamber of our being. We have learned to see, examine, and verify things in the external world, but we have not learned to practice to know all the dimensions of our life. Ishvara is our very soul. When the ego is purified or made aware of the Reality, of the eternal presence of Ishvara within, then self-surrender becomes spontaneous. When the mere self—body, senses, breath, and mind—becomes an instrument or channel for the center of Consciousness (Ishvara), then self-surrender is achieved. Attainment through self-surrender is one of the highest paths. Fortunate are those who have surrendered themselves to the mighty Self.

Self-surrender is considered to be the highest of all yogas. In this path the yogic exercises and other techniques like concentration and meditation are not involved. The yoga of self-surrender has been explained by Lord Krishna in the eighteenth chapter of the Bhagavad Gita. According to this method of attainment, the aspirant surrenders all that he has— his body, mind, intellect, and ego—entirely to the Lord of life in order to establish truth and supreme bliss. Two qualities of action lead the aspirant to self-surrender: faithfulness and sincerity. Faithfulness is to admit and to manifest no movement other than that which is promoted by the innermost conscious-ness. Sincerity requires the lifting of all movements of mind, body, and action to the level of the highest consciousness where the thought of individuality or duality ceases. Sincerity is one of the qualities that aspirants should cultivate with all efforts. Those who surrender without reserve, to them Atman reveals itself. Desire for self-surrender and mere assumptions of mental attitude do not help much in this path. When total surrender is accomplished, the entire personality is transformed. Without complete self-surrender, it is not possible to attain the Divinity. In the process of self-surrender, the student opens himself to the divine force and allows it to work through his mind, action, and speech. Divine grace and bliss are ever-present, but the human ego creates a wall and resists this force because of the ignorance he develops with the association of the mind, which flows to the external world with the help of the senses. Mind has its own ideas and always clings to them. It has its habits and always flows to the grooves of its habits. The ego controls the life of the ignorant; he lives in the world that is ruled by ego. Unless there is a burning desire to go beyond, self-surrender is impossible. Self-surrender should be unconditional. Self-surrender is the way of accepting the divine with the whole heart and mind. It is the shortest of all paths, yet very difficult and very easy also. The Ishopanisad declares, *"Tena tyaktena";* that is, the way of practicing self-surrender is to "offer all the fruits of thy actions and then enjoy."

Asana

In the beginning, the observances, or commitments, of yoga seem to be very difficult, but once a student decides and determines to follow the path, he will find them easy and delightful. One's concept toward one's whole life becomes completely different than it was before.

When one is prepared, when he is committed to follow his path, then he goes to the third rung, which is called asana, posture, or pose. Just as there are two sets of commitments, there are also two sets of asanas—those of physical culture and those of meditative culture. Those postures that help one to become supple, to have control over his body and body gestures, to build his body and keep him free of disease and ill health are called postures of physical culture. The yogis learned many of these postures from the animals, birds, insects, and even from trees. There are many thousands of these postures, but out of these, only eighty-four are recognized as well-known yoga postures. For example, the sun salutation is traditionally not considered a yoga posture. The hatha yoga system was systematized only a hundred years ago by a yogi named Atmananda Suri. In the Western world, people think that postures alone are hatha yoga and that hatha yoga alone is yoga. Those who do not understand what yoga means, mistakenly think that anyone who does certain postures is a yogi. All the postures, all the *kriyas* or washes, all the *mudras* or hand positions, all the *bandhas* or locks that are directly related to the body are a part of *asana,* the third rung of astanga yoga. It is a preventive method of keeping the body healthy.

Postures of physical culture are very important in helping one to have a healthy body, but there is another set of postures that is used for meditation. All the physical postures help the aspirant to find one posture that can make him comfortable and steady at the same time. In the meditative posture, the student learns to be comfortable in a seated position that is easy and at the same time helps to make him steady and comfortable, with his head, neck, and trunk in a straight line. Most people think that posture means doing certain exercises, but actually, posture means learning to have control over one's body, its language, gestures, and movements. No other method of physical exercise can be compared with the yoga postures, for yoga postures make the body supple and strong. When one starts working with his body by practicing postures, he becomes aware of another dimension of life: that he is not body alone. He is a breathing being too. He wants to learn breathing exercises. After learning breathing exercises, awareness leads the student to higher dimensions of life, and then he starts learning about his mind and its modifications. When one learns to do concentration and meditation, then he becomes aware of a higher level of life, the center of consciousness from where consciousness flows on various degrees and grades. In this way, the yoga postures lead the student to a higher dimension of life. But other exercises do not create such awareness. Other exercises are limited to the muscle life only, while the yogic exercises help one to have control over body, breath, nervous system, and mind. The yoga postures are designed carefully so that the body remains fit enough to be a healthy instrument for doing meditation and finally attaining samadhi.

First of all the student becomes aware of his own capacity and ability. He gradually practices the postures. The cultural postures are designed to stretch and realign the spine for optimal energy flow on all levels. There is a small number of basic postures that can make up a comprehensive daily practice routine that will systematically limber and vitalize the entire body. These postures do not only affect the muscle system, but the digestive, circulatory, nervous, endocrine, and respiratory systems as well. They stimulate and regulate all the functions of the body. There are standing, sitting, backward bending, forward bending, twisting, and inverted postures.

Two basic standing postures are the tree and the triangle. The tree is a balancing posture that helps one to center the mind and body in perfect equilibrium. The triangle pose allows one to develop flexibility and strength through twisting and stretching. Three backward bending postures—the cobra, locust, and bow—focus on making the spine flexible. The cobra stretches the upper spine, the locust stretches the lower spine, and the bow stretches the entire spine. These poses also have subtle effects on the autonomic nervous system. The flow of blood to the ganglionated cords on either side of the spinal column is regulated by practicing these simple exercises. The posterior stretch, a forward bending pose, is practiced immediately after the backward bending poses to give the spine a stretch in the opposite direction and to balance their effects. In this pose, the digestive system is especially stimulated due to the pressure in the abdominal area. The spinal twist is very beneficial as it provides a gentle massage to all the internal organs. There is one sequence of postures—the plow, shoulderstand, and fish—that regulates the endocrine system and thus enhances overall health. The shoulderstand is called the all-member pose because its influence on the glandular system affects the entire body. This is said to be the queen of all postures, but the headstand is the king. The headstand reverses the pull of gravity and rejuvenates the entire being. The last major posture brings relaxation and tranquility to mind and body both. This is *savasana,* the corpse pose.

These cultural poses prepare one to perfect a meditative posture. Real posture means sitting still. The Bible explains it in a nutshell—"Be still and know that I am God." Asana is that which makes one still. Any posture that makes one steady, comfortable, and straight is the proper posture. There are only three or four meditative postures, and one cannot discover any new ones. So much research has already been done on this for several thousand years that the yogis tell the students not to waste their time on researching this point. One cannot do the headstand and meditate; one cannot do the peacock and meditate. Many students ask, "Can I lie down?" That is also a posture, and it is very comfortable and steady. But after some time one will go to sleep, so it is not recommended.

Padmasana means the lotus posture. This is actually not used by the accomplished yogi for meditation, but is a therapeutic posture. This is a symbolic posture. As a lotus grows in the mud and lives above, one should live like a lotus in the world. I have never seen any Western student who could apply this posture accurately. Even those who have taught yoga for many years cannot do this posture correctly. There is also one common defect inherent in this posture. When one applies it, he cannot apply *mulabandha* (the root lock) along with it. A more useful posture is called *siddhasana,* or the accomplished pose. The heel of the left foot should be at the perineum, and the right foot should be tucked in between the thigh and calf. Yogis use this accomplished pose and perfect it, but it is said that if one does this posture in excess—for more than two hours at a time—after three to six months, he will lose his desire for sex. So it's not healthy for people of the world to do it for more than two hours. A yogi should apply a meditative posture for at least three hours and thirty-four minutes at a time. When he is able to have a steady posture for three hours and thirty-four minutes, he can then attain samadhi. Another posture is *svastikasana,* the auspicious posture. For this posture, one starts with the right foot, but for the accomplished posture, one begins with the left foot. Here, the heels are symmetrical, and the ankles should not rest on each other but should rest in the hollow of one another so they don't create any pressure or stress. In padmasana, the heels dig into the cavity of the abdomen, but here one doesn't have to do that; one rests them on the inside of the thighs. There is another asana called the easy pose, *sukhasana.* It is the simple crosslegged posture where the calf muscles are rested on the ankles.

One must gradually practice and develop the flexibility to sit in these postures for meditation. He should not force himself into them or he will hurt his ligaments, muscles, and cartilage. Instead, one can sit on a chair with his feet flat on the floor and his hands on his knees. This is also a yogic pose. It is called *maitreyasana,* the friendship posture. The first requirement for a meditative pose is that it is steady, and second is that it is comfortable. For steadiness the head, neck, and trunk should be in a straight line. Why should they be in a straight line? If one feels comfortable slumped forward, why can't he meditate that way? On both sides of the spinal column lie ganglionated cords, and if one does not allow those cords to function properly, if the flow along them is disturbed or disrupted, his nervous system cannot function as it should. So one should learn to keep his spine comfortable and straight.

Pranayama

In the hatha yoga system pranayama seems more important than practicing postures, washes, mudras, and bandhas. Pranayama is the fourth rung of astanga yoga. *Prana* means the vital force; *yama* means control. With the help of certain breathing exercises, the student learns to control, direct, and establish harmony in the pranic vehicles, which are many, but there are ten main ones. Out of the ten, *prana* and *apana,* inhalation and exhalation, are two main breaths that are trained to regulate the motion of the lungs, for the lungs are the storehouse of the intake and output of pranic energy.

It is interesting to observe the functions of these two breaths, which constantly guard the interest of the city of life. It is true that breath is life, and without breath, no one can survive. The yogis learn to understand the subtlemost behavior of the breath, and by regulating the breath, they learn to control their minds.

Pranavedins have a separate school that proclaims that it is a complete science in itself and all other paths are merely speculations. But such yogis are rare and to tread this path one needs strict discipline throughout life. But it is important for all students to understand, know, and practice a few important exercises, which enable them to know their pranic vehicles. The pranic vehicle, or the sheath of energy, is more subtle than the physical body. It is a bridge between the mind and body. In the systematic study of raja yoga, exercises like *nadi shodhanam, kapalabhati, brahmari, puraka, rechaka,* and *kumbhaka* purify and strengthen the energy channels and nervous system. When a student has learned to work with his physical body, then he finds the necessity of working with his nervous system and the channels through which pranic energy flows.

Because of our defective living and bad habits, we disrupt the behavior of our breath, and when the inhalation and exhalation is disturbed, the capacity of the lungs decreases and the pumping station (heart) does not supply sufficient blood to the brain. The brain, being the seat of the mind, is not at rest when disturbed. Therefore pranayama exercises are important for mental equilibrium too. The student learns to sit in a quiet, clean, and airy place and to regulate the motion of the lungs during inhalation and exhalation.

There are a few simple pranayama exercises that will give the student energy, clarity of mind, and even emotional maturity. In the bellows breath the student rapidly exhales and inhales, expelling air from the lungs by dynamic motion of the abdomen and diaphragm. This is not to be confused with hyperventilation, which involves rapid, shallow chest breathing and is indicative of high anxiety. The bellows breath cleanses the lungs and increases one's level of energy. It empties the alveoli of used up gases, especially carbon dioxide.

Nadi shodhanam, or channel purification, is one of the finest pranayama exercises that the student can practice. Its benefits are vast. Here the student alternates the flow of air through the nostrils. In nadi shodhanam the subtle energy channels, ida and pingala, are purified and brought to a state of equilibrium. This balanced state, in which air flows equally through both nostrils, is called sushumna. This state of calm and alert tranquility is essential for the successful practice of meditation. If the student practices nadi shodanam for five to ten minutes, three times a day, his emotional life will become balanced and his nervous system will be purified. It is an excellent exercise for those who have had traumatic experiences or who have misused medications or drugs in the past.

Many books and teachers in the West tell students that if they want to speed up their progress, they should practice kumbhaka, retention of the breath. And many students eagerly adopt this procedure. This can be very dangerous, however, and competent teachers never prescribe such practices to unprepared students. Practicing retention without proper preparation and guidance can cause serious damage to the vital sheath, which can result in disease and even death. The practice of retention intensifies the effects of one's state of mind. If one is tranquil and balanced, this is very beneficial. But if one is negative and extreme, it creates many problems. Kumbhaka should only be practiced if it is individually prescribed and demonstrated by a highly competent teacher.

The first four rungs of the yoga ladder constitute the hatha yoga system. In the word *hatha, ha* and *tha* are the symbols for ida and pingala, left and right breaths. Therefore, hatha yoga is comprised of physical exercises and pranayama both. As the first four rungs constitute the system of hatha yoga, the last four rungs constitute the system of raja yoga. Some students think that it is not necessary for them to practice hatha yoga in order to follow raja yoga, and others say that all the steps of yoga should be followed literally.

Pratyahara, Meditation, and Concentration

The next rung of the yoga ladder is pratyahara, which means "learning to withdraw the senses voluntarily from the objects of the world." There is no literature available on pratyahara, but this rung is very important and should be properly understood and practiced, especially to attain samadhi. Samadhi is not possible without practicing pratyahara.

The student of meditation, without understanding the importance of pratyahara, cannot concentrate the mind and thus is unable to sit in meditation. The mind is in the habit of functioning along ten avenues or senses. These senses distract and dissipate the energy of mind. But the mind can function without the help of the senses. In such a state, the mind starts turning within. During the practice of pratyahara, the student restrains himself from doing meaningless actions that are not related to this practice. Learning to withdraw the senses from the objects of the world does not mean withdrawal from the world, but the student, before sitting in meditation, has to learn to withdraw the senses from the objects of sense perception before he steps into another stage called concentration. Here I would like to mention that concentration for meditation and concentration in the external world are two different ideas. Concentration in the external world does not help the student of meditation.

Paying attention toward the action one is performing

and performing one action at a time strengthens the power of concentration. Concentration helps one to be successful in the external world by helping him to do his duties efficiently and competently. It should not be forgotten that the mind attends one thing at a time, though at a fast speed. Students often think that the mind can attend more than one thing at a time. In attempting this, the power of distraction increases and concentration decreases. For strengthening concentration, attention should be trained. That is why the teacher gives an object or a point—to focus the mind for strengthening concentration. A fully concentrated mind has immense power—unbelievable power—which is attained by concentrating and focusing the mind. That makes the mind one-pointed, and pratyahara makes the mind inward. The inward tendency and one-pointedness help the student in doing meditation. In meditation, the mind starts flowing spontaneously and uninterruptedly, but this flow of concentrated mind is inward. The body remains still, and the breath remains calm and serene. Such a mind experiences the joys of meditation.

So often, students learn to sit in meditation without preliminary preparations and are disappointed if they do not find peace of mind and joy in meditation. Actually, according to the system of raja yoga, the student needs to prepare himself before he practices meditation. In our day-to-day life, and from our childhood onward, sitting still, looking within, withdrawing the senses, and focusing the mind on the centers (like the space between the eyebrows and the center between the breasts) are not taught. Therefore it is difficult for a student to actually meditate and find the inexplicable joy that is quite different from the joy derived from the pleasures of the world. The joy derived out of meditation makes one calm, balanced, and thoughtful. Such a joy gives strength to students, and they remain undisturbed in the trials of life. In order to form such a habit of being undisturbed—even by strong memories and imaginations—one must at first choose a calm, quiet place for meditation.

Meditation opens an entirely new dimension of life for the student. There is no other method for enjoying *now* except the method of meditation. When meditation deepens, and the mind starts flowing toward the center of consciousness, then the student finds great delight, and meditation becomes a part of life. When one learns to sit regularly, at the same exact time and place, he gradually expands his capacity, and his mind forms a habit and finds delight in meditation. Much has been written on the subject, but very little is useful, for inner experiences cannot be drawn on a piece of paper. It is important that the student of meditation is guided, at least for some time until his meditation is strengthened, and that he receives instructions from a teacher who has direct experience and who himself practices meditation. Many obstacles obstruct the student when he encounters his memories, symbols, and ideas. Sometimes the fancies and fantasies are mistaken for visions. Some students are deluded by extraordinary visions, and some aspire to experience and visualize something extraordinary. Neither of these types of students progress, because the psychic world bewilders and distracts them. Students should learn to reject such experiences and watch their progress by the signs and symptoms of calmness, clarity, and one-pointedness. If there is no sign or symptom of calmness, balance, and clarity of mind in the personality of the student, there is something wrong with the method of meditation. Anyone can theoretically know the method of meditation in a matter of a half hour, but practice alone is the real method of learning.

As in the external world there are many charms and temptations, similarly, the experiences of meditation in the preliminary stage can completely disillusion the student. For example, when a student tries to concentrate the conscious part of mind and then penetrates into the levels of the unconscious, he he finds himself lost, sometimes afraid, and most of the time brooding on the past. In such cases, the teacher helps him to cross the ocean of confusion created by the past memories. By pratyahara sense perceptions are controlled, and by concentration the mind is directed toward a definite point of concentration. But by meditation the mind is led beyond all the levels of the unconscious.

What does one search for in meditation? It is foolish to search for anything extraordinary or to desire to visualize something. The student should determine that his mind does not go back to the old grooves of his habits. It needs constant vigilance, determination, and inner strength. All the obstacles pass away if one persists. Here I would like to mention a very important point for the benefit of students. The mind, as it is, is full of images, and visualization of one particular image will definitely strengthen concentration.

Careful study at this point reveals that the mind should either meditate with the help of a mantra, a sound syllable, or a tiny light not as big as the size of the thumb. Visualizing colors or any object could be useful for concentration, but never for meditation. Meditating on the sound of a mantra can lead one to the soundless state, and thus a deep state of silence. Focusing the mind on a certain chakra (spiritual center) hastens the process of meditation. Many exercises of relaxation should not be thought of as part of meditation. Relaxation exercises are for releasing stress, but the meditation method, if systematically practiced, releases stress, removes many psychological disorders, and leads to a deeper state of happiness. It should be remembered that anything we have seen, heard, studied, or imagined can alone distract the mind, and one has not to repeat all this in meditation, but should make mental efforts to go beyond. Here, beyond means within. The senses are beyond the body, and the mind is beyond the senses. The center of Consciousness is beyond the mind. Beyond the mind does not mean beyond human grasp, but beyond all states of mind.

There is nothing external that can help the student in attaining a deeper state of meditation, but the external world can definitely distract one and thus create obstacles for the meditator. His own mind, will power, and determination help him to attain the next step, samadhi. The purpose of meditation is to be constantly aware of the center of consciousness within. A human being is like a finite vessel, and within him dwells infinity. Students, by being aware of infinity, can practice meditation in their daily actions. This method of meditation can be termed meditation in daily life or meditation in action. But in the beginning, it is important to train oneself to sit still and follow the meditational discipline. Those who, for any reason, cannot practice meditation in silence, can practice meditation amidst their duties.

Some of the dedicated students of samadhi who have completely devoted their lives to the meditative practices simultaneously practice *yoga nidra.* This is like the practice of meditation, yet it is different from meditation and definitely helps in strengthening the meditation method.

The human mind is a vast reservoir of creative potentials. It can explore many dimensions of life, provided it is trained to do so. The researchers of the interior world—yogis—know how to go to deep sleep and wake up with the help of their *sankalpa shakti,* or the faculty of determination. This sort of sleep is called yoga nidra. The quality of rest that one derives out of this technique is far superior to, and more useful than, ordinary sleep. Ordinary sleep gives partial rest, while yoga nidra gives total rest to the body and the conscious mind. Dreaming may be therapeutic in many ways, but dreams that consume sleeping hours are never healthy. Waking, dreaming, and sleeping are the states of mind, and if mind is trained by the practice of yoga nidra, one can consciously go to deep sleep and wake up without being haunted by nightmares and fearful dreams.

Here I am not condemning or discarding the validity of dream therapy, but for the student of yoga nidra, it is time-consuming and a stumbling block in their practice. A dream is an expression of the mind in which suppression and repression are expressed. These suppressions find the opportunity to express themselves during the dreaming state, but yoga nidra is a practice of taking full rest by consciously going to a deep state of sleep. Those who have control over this urge can go to deep sleep and wake up whenever they want. To complain all the time that, "I am tired and do not sleep well," is a lazy man's philosophy. If one learns how to give rest to his muscle life first, and then how to purify his nerve channels, not allowing carbon dioxide or used up gas to be retained in the system, then his toxin-free body will be in a healthy state. Then the conscious mind can be withdrawn from sense activities and put into a state of rest.

Samadhi

Concentration leads to one-pointedness, prolonged concentration leads to meditation, and through meditation the mind expands into the superconscious state, which is called samadhi. Patanjali, however, warns us that the practice of concentration must be accompanied by nonattachment, for one who tries to concentrate while remaining attached to the things of the world will either fail altogether, or his acquired power of concentration will lead him into great danger because he will use it for selfish ends.

There are two stages of samadhi. In *savikalpa samadhi,* the first stage, one retains his sense of individuality. The seeker of truth sees the Truth, but retains his sense of "I" as being different from the Truth realized. He has to go beyond savikalpa samadhi to the stage of *nirvikalpa samadhi* in which the seeker becomes one with the Absolute. Here is to be found the union of Atman with Brahman. This stage transcends the stage of intense love and longing for the ideal, for now the seeker merges into his ideal, and no sense of duality remains.

Only one who is well-established in the stage of nirvikalpa samadhi is an illumined yogi, and only he can truly guide other aspirants. Such a yogi is beyond the bondage of space, time, and causation, and he is ever free, for it is possible for him to remain one with Brahman and yet to return to normal consciousness. He has achieved eternal bliss.

Even during sleep a yogi remains fully awake to Brahman, and in the waking state he remains as if asleep to worldly attachments. In this divine union, the subject and the object are dissolved in an ocean of supreme love. It is difficult to express the joy of this superconscious state. Personal experience is the only way to realize that eternal joy.

The word *samahitam*, which means "the state where all of one's questions are resolved," conveys the experiential quality of the state of samadhi. When all the questions are resolved and there is no doubt of any sort, then such a mind soars high beyond the level of the languages in which it is accustomed to think. Samadhi is not on the level of thinking or even feeling, and this is why it is also called *bhavatita*, which means "beyond." The state of samadhi, according to Patanjali's system, is considered to be the highest state attainable by yogis.

In other schools the word samadhi is not used. The meditative school of Buddhism, for instance, uses the word *nirvana* to describe the highest state of consciousness—through negation one experiences a void, which is called nirvana. The school of advaita philosophy describes it as we have already explained in the chapter, "Jnana Yoga." According to raja yoga, when the individual consciousness expands itself to cosmic consciousness, when jiva unites itself to the Ishvara, then the word samadhi is used. It is a state beyond. It is the eighth, and final, rung on the yoga ladder and is achieved when the aspirant establishes his practice firmly: when he is able to continue his meditation for a long time without interruption and with full devotion and reverence, and when the subtle sense of self-identity vanishes, allowing control of the latent modifications of the mind. Then samadhi is attained.

Samadhi is not a state that can be attained easily, but if one achieves it, supramental knowledge, or intuitional knowledge, is experienced—and one who does not possess this cannot understand the mysteries of life. In this state of the senses, mind and intellect cease functioning, and, just as a river merges into the ocean, so does the individual soul merge into the supreme soul—and all limitations disappear. Beginners are often afraid of this union because they think that their individualities might dissolve or be engulfed. Actually, what occurs is not a loss of individuality, but an expansion of individuality. As long as the individual mind functions within the limited realms of individual consciousness, one can meditate, but he can never attain samadhi. The deepest state of meditation, however, expands individual consciousness, and when it has been expanded to its fullest capacity, that is called samadhi. It can also be termed "sleepless sleep." This superconscious state is called turiya, or the "fourth state." The first three states (waking, dreaming, and dreamless sleep) are experienced by everyone. When a yogi establishes himself in the fourth state he experiences the living Reality. Then he realizes, at all times and under all circumstances, that he is identical with existence, knowledge, and bliss (*sat, chit,* and *ananda*). Real spiritual life begins after one enters into this state of superconsciousness. It is the state of divine peace. In this state the Divine meets Divine and remains one, free from all pains, miseries, and bondages.

Chapter
6

Laya Yoga

The Path of Fusion

The path of laya yoga is practiced by the aspirants who have a profound knowledge of raja yoga, Samkhya philosophy, and Tantra philosophy. Those who have understood the importance of unveiling all the mysteries of life follow this path. The Sanskrit word *laya* means dissolution and fusion. It denotes the processes that occur on different levels of reality. In laya yoga, the unfolding of these levels of life is done in a systematic way through Self-unveiling, Self-revelation, and Self-realization.

An aspirant seeks to dissolve the personal universe and to gradually dissolve the ties that bind him consciously or unconsciously, knowing that all the components of his personality finally go to decay and decomposition. He endeavors to master the principles that are active in the processes of composition and also gains the knowledge of those principles that decompose his individuality. Just as the phenomena and organization of the universe disintegrate in order to reintegrate by the laws of nature, so the aspirant makes voluntary efforts to disintegrate the phenomena within his individuality in order to reintegrate by his voluntary concentrated efforts. The method for attaining this dissolution is called *laya yoga*.

Laya yoga, like kundalini yoga, leads the student from the gross to the subtle, and then to the most subtle aspect of consciousness. It is like a process of filtration. This spiritual voyage is not that of Atman or the pure spiritual Self. That which was never born is not subject to death. No dissolution or reintegration can occur in Atman, which is self-existent and eternal in its nature. Dissolution and reintegration can occur only in the layer of personality, which is but a manifestation of the integration of many evolutes of matter. Atman is deeply hidden inside the coverings of veils and sheaths. These sheaths are physical, pranic, mental, intellectual, and blissful. Atman, the center of consciousness, radiates its light through these veils and sheaths, permeating each and suffusing it with the force of life. At each level, or sheath, the pure Self, Atman, or the center of consciousness, becomes identified by the name given to that particular level of reality. When it permeates the mind, the ignorant think that the mind is the true Self; when it imbues the body with the life force, the ignorant feel that the body is the true Self.

The aspirant makes full effort to dispel the darkness created by such confusion by cutting the bondage of super-impositions and misidentifications so that the light of pure Atman is realized. Without the realization of this light, the student identifies himself with those levels of life that only give him a partial glimpse of the light, and never the whole.

The goal of the laya yogins is to retrace the steps of realization systematically in order to uncover the center of consciousness from where consciousness flows on various degrees and grades. It is like grasping the light of the sun with the help of a sunbeam and gradually climbing to the corona and then into the heart of the sun. As a sunbeam passes through many impeding wraps that must be dissolved and disintegrated, so the aspirant practices this path to pass through the sheaths in the upward journey to the very source and fountain of life.

Laya yoga incorporates all of the processes of this voyage of the principle of awareness from the relatively gross, coarse, dense, slowly vibrating phenomena to the respectively finer, subtler, faster vibrating interior energies. When the principle of awareness, in deep concentration of will, dissolves a bond of identity and attains freedom from the bondage of veils, then laya means "dissolution." It can be termed "fusion" when the awareness infuses its greater intensity of power in a veil, making the veil a transparent conductor of Reality. Then laya means infusion, absorption, and assimilation. It uplifts the gross to the subtle, the lower to the higher, and finally transforms the whole of individuality. This is a reversal of the reversal, a return to the source. Ordinarily the ignorant are aware of the external flow of consciousness, but with the practice of laya yoga, the aspirant starts to flow in the eternal stream of inward consciousness, or *pratyaka chetna adhigamah* (Yoga Sutras, I.29), as opposed to the outward flow of the senses into the mere kinetic motion of the world of phenomena.

The path of laya yoga is usually followed by those who have acquired the knowledge of all the sheaths, the energy that flows respectively from the subtlemost to the grossest level of life. Before treading this path, the aspirant studies the fundamentals of the scriptures and understands his relationship with the universe. This pursuit of knowledge is followed by the students of cosmology.

We will describe the methods of practice in the section explaining the awakening of the primal force, which remains sleeping at the base of the spinal column. The laya yoga process is not random but requires a methodical approach. The great masters of yoga science fully understood the relationship of cause and effect as described in the system of Samkhya philosophy. The lines of the grid of consciousness, known as *yantra,* pass through these interrelationships of cause and effect. Actually, laya yoga establishes a profound synthesis of the Samkhya and Tantric philosophies and practices.

Samkhya philosophy views all matter and nature as a single system. The components of individuality are the same as those in the rest of the universe. A human being's individual universe is subject to the same laws that govern the larger universe outside him. One of these laws is the law of evolution and involution of elements.

According to Samkhya philosophy, there is a certain order in which the phenomena of the universe, including the material aspect of the personality, evolved. This order is accepted by most schools of Eastern philosophy:

> *mahat* and *buddhi:* the cosmic and individual intelligence
> *ahankara:* ego, the identifying principle

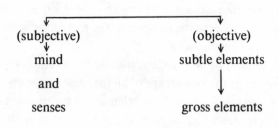

This is the order of evolution from the subtlemost to the grossest aspect of the universe. The order of involution or dissolution is the opposite. The yogi begins with the mastery of the grossest elements with which his mind has identified. He first learns to free himself from the visible chains of bondage, and then proceeds upward to the finer levels of consciousness, and then to the finest.

The ego principle is divided into subjective and objective.

The subjective observes, experiences, and controls the objective. The mind and the senses are employed to experience the elements and are therefore superior to the elements. Human beings experience the external phenomena because the mind and senses interpret them. This causes us to view the world as a five-fold reality of earth, water, fire, air, and space. These are called *tattvas*. According to this philosophy, space is not a void but is a form of matter just like the mind. If we consider mahat. ahankara, and mind to be the three-fold subjective principle, we can place all three categories under a single term—mind, with the senses as its instruments. The mind is the subtlest of all material phenomena. It is a finer energy of the universe. conditioned only by space and time. Similarly, its energy is reduced in vibratory frequency progressively from space all the way down to the earth element.

The reader should note that this description is not meant to explain how the external physical universe is produced, but rather it is intended to explain how pure Consciousness radiates its brilliance to the surface of the body. The center of Consciousness radiates its light to the mind first and the mind extends to space and experiences all that is produced from space and is held therein. The entire chain of causation is thus touched by the illumination of consciousness. This is the reversal of consciousness from inward to outward flow. The yogi dissolves the earth element into water, water into fire, fire into air, air into space, space into mind, and mind—with ego and intelligence—into *prakriti,* which is the unmanifest and the subtlemost intangible cause of the natural phenomena. The phenomenalization of awareness ceases here, but this does not mean that the body, which partakes of the five elements and houses the mind, ceases, nor that the yogi becomes mindless. It means that the yogi's awareness expands and is no longer bound to mere physical surfaces or to the sensations that are channeled through the senses. Interaction with sense objects still takes place, but attachment to them vanishes.

It is said that one fallen in the mud must begin his attempts to get up by putting his hand in that very mud. Thus, the laya yogi, interested in dissolving the chain of bondage, begins with concentrations on the earth element. A digger gets dusty and mud-splattered in the act of digging a well, but in the end, he washes off his dust and mud with the water of the very well he got dusty digging.

The yogi dissolves his earth attachment into the water principles and continues the process until the mind itself is dissolved into its origin, prakriti. Taking earth for the start, numerous methods of concentraion are practiced on each of these elements.

An aspirant may focus his senses on the earthly form until his mind is fully concentrated and roving thoughts vanish. The object of concentration could be a square, a circle, or a *linga* (image). One must become completely absorbed in contemplation of the object concentrated upon. As a result, both expansion and absorption occur. In expansion, the material universe is understood, but in absorption, the yogi experiences the inner levels of life. First he learns to master the physical body through specific physical and mental exercises. Then all the attributes of the mental qualities that relate to the earth element are brought under control. It is stated that the sense of smell is experienced when he concentrates on the earth element. In the scriptures it is written that such mastery of concentration is capable of producing any fragrance desired.

Expansion and absorption are two sides of the same coin. When the mind is fully focused on a prescribed principle in the subtle body, it expands to incorporate all the gross external corresponding forms of that subtle principle. Every element has its quality and when the yogi meditates on the element, he gains mastery over the subtle quality of the element. All five elements have their qualities, but the purpose is to systematically know the qualities of each element from earth to water and upward. By concentrating on water, or listening to the sound of flowing water, the yogi masters all that is water-like in the physical body, and water's corresponding attributes, such as taste. Similar methods are used for the mastery of the other elements. In all cases, the purpose is to master the principles that are internal. The mind's expansion into consciousness of a principle in its universal framework is a natural by-product.

Laya yoga is integrated with the other paths of yoga. Laya yoga and nada yoga are inseparable. The science of mantra is extensively practiced to gain control over the subtle principles corresponding to the elements. Each element is seen in its appropriate *chakra,* or energy center, with its own special color and particular sound seed. The consciousness rising from the lower to the higher causes the grosser element to be dissolved into the next subtler element.

In the system of Patanjali the control of mind and its elements is explained extensively—as the laya of modifications into their causes. The modifications of the mind do not arise without some prior existence. When the control of the mind and its modifications is attained, samadhi ensues. Those who attain this level of consciousness dissolve the phenomenal evolutes into prakriti and experience a void-like state of mind. This state of mind is only a state of *samprajnata samadhi.* Self-realization occurs beyond this laya in *asamprajnata samadhi.*

Laya yoga leads the yogi through the first six levels of consciousness. The final assent to the seventh is explained and described in kundalini yoga. Tantric literature, and especially the Samaya school, leads the student to the realization of the union of *jiva* (embodied soul) and *Shiva* (the supreme Reality) by awakening the primal force. With the help of this force, the yogi is able to penetrate all levels of consciousness and ascends to the highest peak of wisdom.

Chapter 7

Kundalini Yoga

The Path of Primal Force

Kundalini yoga is the most advanced and technical path in which a definite methodology is followed strictly. The word *kundalini* comes from the word *kundala,* which means "coiled." There is also another word, *kunda,* meaning "bowl," which is used for sacrificial fire. In the kunda, the primal fire called kundalini resides. The image of a serpent-like fire resting at the root of the spinal column conveys the idea of kundalini. This primal force is the coiled-up power at the perineum of the human body.

Kundalini gently shines, enhaloed with a mass of golden light. It is self-illuminated, lying in an intoxicated state, coiled three and a half times with its tail in its mouth, covering with its face the entrace of sushumna—*brahmarandhra.* That is why it is symbolized as a serpent fire. The ultimate success of all yoga practices depends upon the awakening of kundalini.

The object of yoga practice is to awaken and lead the primal force, kundalini, upward through sushumna. There are many other methods (like complete dedication, self-surrender, and intense devotion) for awakening kundalini, but the systematic way that the tantric literature explains is a very scientific way of awakening kundalini. The path of jnana yoga, when contemplation is intensified by the study of the scriptures under the guidance of a competent teacher, can also arouse kundalini. In fact, any spiritual practice that leads to a general awakening and experience of transcendent states of consciousness involves an awakening of this latent force.

Kundalini is a burning topic for modern writers, but their writings are completely misleading. The modern literature available on this subject, although full of references and quotations, has very little worthwhile material because of its absence of practicality. For this reason, it is a difficult task to awaken kundalini without the help of a competent teacher. An accomplished teacher can shorten the process; otherwise, it takes a long time. So before students start practicing the path of kundalini yoga, they should examine their teacher and personally find out whether he is accomplished in this science, or whether he just instructs on the basis of the information he has received from others. Spiritual mockery is most dangerous and injurious.

The false claims of arousing the power of kundalini in students through mere touch, presence, or gaze is absolutely misleading. The unprepared student aspires to have a magic-maker as his teacher. He does not want to learn, study, understand, or practice. All that he finally achieves is the illusion of power and never the real experience of bliss. Without long and sincere practice of purification and without expanding one's own capacity, the flood of energy could disorient and confuse the student, and on the physical level, such a charge of energy could threaten the integrity of the body. But through careful training, the student gradually learns to master his deep-rooted habit patterns and prepares himself to face the full awakening of the energy that lies latent within him.

In all great mystic traditions of the world, there have been experiences of awakening this latent force, such as the experience of Moses before the burning bush and of Mohammed on the night of power when the teachings of the Koran were revealed to him. The Book of Revelation in Judaism and Christianity is also full of such experiences. Hindu and Buddhist scriptures have extensive literature on the philosophy of tantra and the practices of awakening this primal force. This literature again and again advises the aspirant to study and practice under the guidance of a competent teacher only.

Awakening Kundalini through Hatha Yoga

According to hatha yoga, the kundalini force is awakened by practicing advanced yogic techniques. As long as the roving mind identifies itself with the objects of the world, it is not possible for an aspirant to understand and be aware of the various levels of human consciousness. He who awakens this power enters on the path that releases him from all bonds of ignorance.

The most advanced hatha yoga system states that the nervous system furnishes the physiological basis of this aspect of yoga, and without its knowledge it is impossible to awaken this sleeping force.

When kundalini is aroused, it is systematically led through the chakras in successive stages by giving life and motion to these subtle centers in the spinal column, which normally remain latent. However, these chakras are not physical plexuses but subtle centers, though they correspond to and are located according to the position of the plexuses. It is only the power of kundalini that can pierce these subtle centers and reach the *brahmarandhra*. Students who are able to awaken and lead the kundalini become very creative and dynamic.

Kundalini is the highest manifestation of consciousness and is the very source of creativity in the universe as well as in the human being. Ordinarily, creation is from spirit to matter, but with the help of yoga practices, the yogi reverses this process and seeks to change matter to spirit, to stay the natural outward movement and return to its source. This primal force is the grand potential. This power embodies all powers and assumes all forms. Therefore, it is the very seat of all bodily and mental operations.

Pranic forces are but the manifestation of kundalini, the static energy of the body. There first must be a neutral center for all manifestations of energy. All the forces that emanate from this neutral point traverse the whole body form and return to it, just as electrical energy runs out of the positive pole of a battery and returns to it by the negative pole. This central part of the body is said to be the reflected neutral center of manifestation of all forces that flow from the brain in the living human frame. As magnetism is latent at the central part of a magnet, so is it in the body center.

In the rotating wheel of life, kundalini may be linked to the imperceptible motion at the axle, the sweep of the periphery being respiration. The energy that comes into respiration has three aspects: neutral, centripetal, and centrifugal. In the nervous system, centripetal currents are called afferent currents, and centrifugal are called efferent currents. These currents have their neutral state in the *muladhara* (anal) chakra, where kundalini remains in a dormant form. By centripetal currents, nutrients and oxygen are taken in, and by centrifugal, waste matters are expelled. The force of energy that is at the back of all manifestations of the nerve force must not be mistaken for the functions of the brain or heart. The scriptures say that kundalini resides at the upper border of the triangular piece of bone of the spinal column between the hip bones, which is known as the sacrum. It is in the center between the navel center and the sex organ and above the perineum, situated in muladhara chakra, which is about four finger breadths square, facing backward. According to yoga scriptures, this space is the root from where the seventy-two thousand channels of energy (*nadis*) arise and flow.

Kundalini is the mother of three qualities: *sattva, rajas,* and *tamas.* Sattva means self-existent, light, lumination, and a source of peace and bliss. Rajas is a quality that makes one active and energetic and motivates one toward actions. Tamas means darkness, sloth, or ignorance. It is the obstructive quality in human unfoldment. These constructive, regulative, and destructive qualities are sattva, rajas, and tamas, accordingly. This static or potential energy, the central powerhouse of the body, is the fountainhead of knowledge that gives birth to our body vehicle, and this is the very center from which the mind is born. From kundalini, the *agni,* the Promethean fire of life, becomes augmented. From the seed of kundalini arises physical energies: *bindu,* the seed of life, and *nada,* sound, the very source of speech.

Kundalini is not manifested as physical sound or vibration but as a most subtle form of spiritual illumination, being the mother of all manifestations. This is the most supreme power. Just as all powers of the universe exist in the unmanifested self-existent Brahman, so do all the powers of the individual exist in kundalini. It is this force that mainly underlies the wonders performed by the yogi. By practicing the awakening of kundalini according to the hatha yoga system, one establishes complete control over his body. All passions and emotions are brought completely under control. Seminal production and reabsorption can only be perfectly balanced after the full awakening of kundalini, and eventually the power of orderly control of all vital functions is acquired. In the more advanced states, the whole body sinks into the deepest lethargy, resembling that which actually precedes death. The advanced student of kundalini yoga learns the method of separating himself from the body and its consciousness, and he experiences a period of transition exactly like death. He gains this voluntary control with the help of kundalini *shakti,* or power. For such a yogi, dying is an art without any pain or misery. The ignorant suffer, while death is brought under conscious control by a yogi. He can die at his wish and will do so when he finds the body is no longer a fit instrument. When the mortal frame of life is no longer a means, the yogi drops his body consciously, exactly the way one changes a garment.

When the aspirant has purifed his physical body and all his internal states through various spiritual disciplines, then he is prepared to take up this courageous voyage. Preparation for awakening the kundalini is more important than the awakening process itself. The practice of hatha yoga, including washes and breathing exercises, prepares the student to awaken this dormant force. The purpose of hatha yoga is to prepare one for sushumna awakening and to keep the body fit to be an instrument that prevents distractions arising from physical and pranic imbalances. Hatha yoga as a system is very beneficial for preparing the body to be an instrument for pranayama, meditation, and kundalini awakening. But it is only a preparation.

After practicing advanced postures, bandhas, mudras, and pranayama exercises, the aspirant can rechannel the dynamic force of pranayama and use it to awaken the latent energy. Prana, being the regulative force of body and mind, enables the aspirant to control the mind and body at will. The kundalini, normally nurtured through *pingala* (right nostril flow) at dawn and *ida* (left nostril flow) at twilight, remains sleeping at all other times, but by means of special postures and the practice of *kumbhaka* (retention) and mudras, this force is awakened. When sushumna is fully applied, samadhi becomes spontaneous.

The hatha yogins believe that with the help of vigorous pranayama practices, one can awaken and lead kundalini to brahmarandhra, the thousand-petalled lotus (*sahasrara*), and thus attain liberation. But this practice could be injurious, for vigorous pranayama needs a well-balanced body, a nutritious diet, and complete dedication. At the same time, it is important for such a student to remain under the guidance of a yogi who knows this subject and who has practiced the whole process. Such an accomplished yogi is hard to find, but it is said that when the student is prepared, the teacher appears.

By the method of leading pranas through upward traveling, the mind becomes detached, one-pointed, and inward, enjoying meditation. Sushumna is the only passage on which the force of kundalini can travel. By awakening sushumna, the mind is brought under complete control, and the evasion of death becomes possible. While doing vigorous pranayama practices, kundalini leaves the entrance, goes into sushumna, and starts moving. When through breathing exercises and breath awareness sushumna is applied, a real meditative state is attained.

Through our breath, we are related with the universal life principle; when we breathe we mingle with the life force. With specific exercises of pranayama, the upward flow of prana and the downward flow of apana merge. The union of these two pranic currents in the central canal creates intense heat. In the Upanishadic literature, these two pranas are called upper and lower *arni*. By the friction created between these two, the fire is created. Then the latent force is aroused from her potential state and starts flowing upward through brahmarandhra. Breath retention (kumbhaka) generates heat and also, with special impingements, it moves the whole storehouse of energy into motion. The *jalandharabandha* and *mulabandha* control the downward tendencies of apana; *asvini mudra* pushes apana upward. *Uddyanabandha* unites prana and apana and helps them enter into sushumna. Through *shaktichalana* one forces the kundalini power from muladhara upward through the chakras. Thus the unification of prana and apana helps kundalini move upward. To start with, a strictly yogic diet is observed, and celibacy is literally practiced until sushumna awakening is accomplished. In the second step, the body is purified by washes and nadi shodhanam. In the third step, kumbhaka, along with the bandhas and mudras, is perfected. Before kundalini awakens, the yogi experiences a few extraordinary signs and symptoms. These phenomena arise in the form of a mist, smoke, hot air, wind, fire, lightning, crystal, and the moon. They are considered to be *siddhis*, or yogic powers. But the yogis instruct their disciples not to be caught up by these siddhis, for they are obstructions on the path of attainment. These powers are not evil in themselves, but the pseudo-yogis misuse these powers, become egotistical, and thus the downfall begins. These siddhis are the signs and symptoms of progress, and they should never be misused.

Applying Sushumna

Application of sushumna and awakening of kundalini are the two most important aspects of yogic practice before union between jiva and Shiva is accomplished. So often, students complain that their minds rove around and meditation becomes impossible, though they regularly practice the method of meditation. It has often been noticed that without the application of sushumna, the mind is always distracted. Application of sushumna brings a great joy to the mind, and such a joyous mind turns within with the desire to have eternal joy. There are two main practices used to apply sushumna. One is to regulate the ida and pingala by practicing nadi shodhanam at least three times a day. Other practices, like outer and inner kumbhaka, help to establish control over the breath flow.

When one examines the flow of his breath, he will find that one of his nostrils remains active and the other remains passive; the flow changes its course from one to the other. But before the flow of the breath changes its course, sushumna is applied automatically for a few moments. These moments are the calmest and most joyous moments of life, but the yogis expand these moments and consciously apply sushumna as long as they want. *Sandhya* is the word used for this union. When a yogi makes voluntary efforts to establish a union between ida and pingala—moon and sun, night and day—that wedding is called sandhya. The yogis apply this state of sushumna and thus create a meditative joy. The breath and mind are inseparable friends and influence each other with their behavior.

When sushumna is applied, the yogi feels a sensation of fire going to the brain as if a hot current of air is being blown through a tube from its lower end to its upper end. With the force of pranic energy, the *muladhara* and *swadisthana* (genital chakra) vibrate, and the primal force is fully awakened. Once kundalini is awakened, the student constantly remains vigilant and aware of this force. When the students of meditation learn to apply sushumna, then they really start practicing meditation, and meditation becomes a joyful experience. This joy is unlike other external joys. The joy of meditation is the highest one, provided the sushumna is applied first.

Another method of applying sushumna is to concentrate mentally on the point where the upper lip meets the bridge between the nostrils. The scriptures say, *"Nasagre dhyanam kuryat"*—"Meditate at the tip of the nostrils." This is often misunderstood by students and mistaken for the external gaze, which is an entirely different practice. The external gaze is a practice of *trataka* and not sushumna awakening. The student can notice when his breath starts flowing freely through both nostrils, and this symptom is an indication of sushumna awakening. With little effort, if regularly practiced, sushumna can be applied. Awakening sushumna and applying sushumna are one and the same. The yogis bring this under their voluntary control and meditate whenever they want. If the students feel cold sensations on their spinal column or brain, it is a symptom of not practicing accurately.

Other Methods of Pranayama

Kundalini may also be awakened by the following process. While practicing the posterior stretch with the chest on the thighs, the head on the knees, and the thumbs and forefingers grasping the big toes, the yogi inhales through the left nostril and retains the breath while creating tension by pulling the anus and navel together. A cotton ball is also taped on the perineum to apply pressure there. Exhalation is made through the right nostril, and then the entire process is repeated for one hour and thirty minutes, while alternating the nostril that initiates inhalation. This draws kundalini up, causing it to leave the entrance of sushumna, and prana begins to flow into the sushumna nadi. The yogi then places each hand on the abdomen on either side of the navel, holding the ribs firm with the heels of the hands. He then performs nauli from right to left and from left to right for at least forty-five minutes, thus awakening kundalini.

In another method a soft pad is placed in such a position as to exert pressure on the space between the sex organ and the anus. The accomplished pose is used in this method. A few yogis use the lotus posture, but in the lotus posture, they find difficulty in applying mulabandha. The yogi practices *khechari mudra,* in which the tongue is rolled back and placed on the palate. The eyes are one-pointedly fixed between the two eyebrows. Kumbhaka follows this practice with the application of *jalandhara bandha,* the chin lock. The breath is trained to flow through sushumna instead of through ida and pingala.

The primal fire, kundalini, is awakened and led, which enables kundalini to pierce sushumna, and then all the chakras are opened.

Shaktichalana mudra: Sleeping like a serpent fire in the cavity of muladhara when suddenly hit by the *kalagni* (apana *vayu*, or energy principle of air), the kundalini is awakened and starts moving like the minute fibers of the lotus flower. Having a serpentine movement, it shines and dashes through sushumna. *Padmasana* and *siddhasana* are practiced for shaktichalana. In this practice, inhalation is done through the right nostril and jalandhara bandha is applied. The eyes are fixed on the tip of the nose or between the two eyebrows. *Asvini mudra* is applied and then *uddyanabandha*. Then slowly one exhales through the left nostril. This process is repeated again and again. With this process it is said that the serpent power is forced to rise upward. The body starts perspiring heavily, and this perspiration is rubbed gently over it; it is never wiped by a towel. It is said that the students of this path practice this exercise for one and one-half hours regularly.

The diet recommended for this practice by the yogic manuals is rice, milk, sugar cane juice, barley broth, and fruits. Various scriptures vary as far as time limit is concerned for awakening kundalini. One of the scriptures says that if this practice is continued for forty minutes every day, in one year's time the kundalini awakens. The purity of the nadis seems to be the key for success. If the intake and output and the exchange between oxygen and carbon dioxide is regulated with the practices of nadi shodhanam, the clarity of mind is evident. Beginners should practice *bhastrika* pranayama and then nadi shodhanam and then perfect kumbhaka.

Bhramari Kumbhaka—The Beetle-droning *Kumbhaka:* Seated in a tranquil posture, the yogi begins to breathe through both nostrils slowly, gradually increasing his respirations and making them more and more frequent, until he is bathed in perspiration. Then inspiring through both nostrils and making a noise like the male bee, he swallows and retains the breath, following kumbhaka with a slow expiration. This practice is preparatory to *rasandha yoga samadhi.*

Rasandha Yoga Samadhi: After doing bhramari kumbhaka, the breath is slowly expelled while making a buzzing sound like that of a female bee or a bee drunk with the nectar of the flower. This is effected by uttering the sound *ah* as low in the throat as possible, vibrating the palate and practicing until the tone can be made clear, when it will take on the characteristic sound of the bee drone. By placing the mind in the center of this sound, a fixation of the mind will arise and great happiness will ensue. This practice can only be effective when kumbhaka can be maintained for several minute's time. It is best done at midnight in absolute silence.

Murcha Kumbhaka: The distinction of this practice is the use of the chin lock in exhalation. This practice renders the mind passive and induces fainting. While sitting in siddhasana posture, inhalation through both nostrils is performed in such a way as to produce a sound of raining, after which the breath is swallowed. Jalandhara bandha and asvini mudra are then applied. Now with the pressure in the lower abdominal region, the air is slowly expelled and followed with an external kumbhaka. This will cause the mind to swoon, producing a sense of comfort. Should fainting occur, it is certain that kumbhaka is successful. To complete this murcha, shakti chalana must be practiced with it. This practice is particularly effective in producing mental passivity.

Another technique resorted to by those accomplished in breathing practices is to draw the breath in by short gasps until the lungs are distended, the left more than the right. Then the body is pressed so as to bring the pressure upon the heart. This leads to the speedy attainment of perfection in pranayama, more so than with any other method.

Kevala Kumbhaka

In *kevala kumbhaka* the full length of breath is confined in the body, and nothing is allowed to go out. This is absolute control of the breath, absolute suspension. This suspension is performed without any physical or muscular effort. Sushumna becomes free of all impurities and the goal of hatha yoga is accomplished.

Having perfected khechari mudra (swallowing of the tongue) and, living in the regulation subterranean retreat, the yogi reduces his diet to that of rich milk only, living entirely on milk for six whole months. He then begins living on clarified butter and milk for about a week, following which he abstains from all foods for a day or two. Then, consciously counting the number of his respirations, he raises them to twice the normal (roughly thirty respirations per minute) and practices this for a time. Then filling the lungs with air, he closes both nostrils; he presses the glottis backward by the tip of the tongue and swallows the tongue into the fascia. Thus he suspends his breath while at the same time fixing his eyes between the eyebrows or on the tip of the nose. When his mind becomes dead he attains spiritual power. When kumbhaka is completed he should give his mind rest.

This may be performed every three hours, or he may practice it five times a day: early morning, noon, afternoon, twilight, or midnight. Or he may do it three times a day. So long as success is not obtained in kevala, this trance asphyxiation should be kept up and the practice gradually increased until there is samadhi. Thus the yogi produces a state of *manomani*—fixedness of mind—at which time kevala is to be practiced only once a day.

This practice cures all diseases, promotes longevity, removes the darkness of the mind, enlightens the moral nature, purges one from all sins, and awakens the soul. Samadhi is experienced, and the breath becomes absorbed into the cosmic soul. The chitta (consciousness) can be made to go anywhere, and perfection in everything is easily attained. It is necessary to be already skilled in the various practices of breathing to undertake kevala kumbhaka and to be capable of perfect concentration of the mind, going as far as samadhi in which thoughts become visualized.

When the airs are united as one and begin to move in the middle channel, sushumna, the whole of the heart becomes void. The yogi's body becomes glowingly healthy and divine and emits a subtle sweet scent. His posture becomes firm. His yoga thus perfected, he masters the "unheard-of sciences." On his tongue always dances the goddess of learning, and he becomes wise.

The yogi's senses are suspended when he can suspend his respiratory movements for ten minutes and forty-eight seconds. *Dharana* is attained when the breath can be held for twenty-one minutes and thirty-six seconds, and *dhyana* is attained when the breath is held for forty-three minutes and twelve seconds. Samadhi is attained after holding the breath for one hour, twenty-six minutes and twenty-four seconds. These last three states of yoga—concentration, meditation, and samadhi—when synthesized, are known as *samyama*.

When the yogi has accomplished kumbhaka to a length of two and a half to three hours, he will attain extraordinary powers, such as hearing sounds at great distances, seeing objects out of ordinary view, covering long distances quickly, and many phenomena considered impossible. To cease one's practice for these greater accomplishments or to play with these developments, which are but a natural consequence in the process of one's advancement, means certain defeat for the yogi and the end of any further advancement on the path. He may, for the purpose of encouraging other practicing yogis, exhibit to them his accomplishments.

The yogi can conquer the earth element when he can introduce his breath of life in the muladhara and restrain it there for two and a half hours. He can conquer all water when he can introduce his mind and breath of life in swadhisthana and retain it there for two and one-half hours; likewise, the fire in the manipura chakra. He controls air with his breath in the anahata for two and a half hours and space when the breath is made stationary in visuddha. Thus he obtains a knowledge of the five elements, and these elements cannot deter him; he enjoys them constantly, thus meeting the cosmic soul.

When the yogi can restrain his breath for three hours then he is able to combine his soul with the cosmic soul. During this state worldly thoughts of no kind whatsoever cross his mind even for a moment. At this time, his passions become completely passive, and he passes without effort from the things of nature to the divine and universal. He can support himself on one finger, and even travel in space like a cotton tree seed. When he succeeds in restraining his breath for three hours he need practice pranayama but once daily.

The cerebral spinal system is brought under control by awakening kundalini. It is said that superhuman powers are attained by these practices, but to be truthful, my experience is quite different. By such vigorous exercises, one experiences and attains some extraordinary states of mind in which one feels many movements and currents, flashes of light, and sometimes violent sensations on the spinal column and brain. If these extraordinary experiences are called superhuman powers, then I agree. But if superhuman powers are different, then I have no experience of such powers after practicing these methods. I have not felt my consciousness being expanded or attaining any sort of super knowledge while practicing these exercises.

In my opinion, these exercises are but preparations for awakening kundalini. I would like to warn students not to waste their time and energy in using physical techniques for awakening kundalini. I practiced these methods in my youth, but I did not derive much spiritual benefit. Those yogis who have no knowledge of Tantra texts and are not educated think that hatha yoga exercises and pranayama exercises are the only means for awakening kundalini, but that is not true. Sometimes these techniques can injure the nervous system by disrupting the pranic vehicles. Excessive pranayama exercises and mudras can lead to ill health.

Awakening through Practicing Anahata Nada

Anahata nada is the celestial sound heard by the mental ear of a yogi. It is not sound created by external instruments of any kind. When a yogi learns not to hear the external sounds, he starts hearing the internal sounds—nada. In the middle of the night, when there is no sound to be heard, the yogi practices kumbhaka by using *baka mudra*—by closing the ears with the two thumbs, the eyes with the index fingers, the nostrils with the middle fingers, the upper lip with the ring fingers, and the lower lip with the little fingers. He pays one-pointed attention to the center between the two eyebrows. Some yogis visualize a light that changes into many colors and forms, and some start listening to the sounds coming from within. Listening to the nadas, the yogi loses his body consciousness, and his mind becomes inward. These nadas are of ten kinds. The first sound is like the humming of the honey-intoxicated bee; the second is like the melody from a flute; the third is like the ringing of bells at a distance; the fourth is like the sound of a conch shell; the fifth is like the sound of a *vina;* the sixth is like the sound created by the striking together of two pieces of metal used by musicians; the seventh is like the sound of a trumpet; the eighth is like the heavier sound coming from the trumpet blast; the ninth is like the sound of thunder; and the tenth is the anahata sound that resembles the constant sound of a prolonged OM. This is the sound that captures the heart of the nada student.

Anahata nada is the very basis of all music practiced and played all over the world. In all the music of the world, there are only seven key notes. The *Sama Veda* explains extensively the origin of music and its effect on the minds and hearts of the sadhakas. It is said that music can lead the aspirant to a state of samadhi. But such musicians are rare, and they devote their whole lives to this pursuit.

The student of anahata nada can easily make his mind inward and one-pointed, it is true. But there are many cults already in existence who, instead of practicing nada for attaining samadhi, become superstitious and adore their gurus as gods. In this way, the yogic practice of nada disappears, and a guru god appears. There is no philosophy behind this path; unquestioning faith is strengthened by such gurudom. As far as the yogic method of nada is concerned, it is definitely valid, but the guru occupying the position of ultimate Reality is not mentioned in any of the scriptures. It is true that the guru or spiritual guide should be revered, and he is like a boat used in crossing the mire of delusion. A competent guru is a positive means in the path of spirituality, but he is not the end.

A real guru is he who selflessly guides his students and makes them aware of the Reality. A selfish person can never become a real guru. It has become a custom among modern students that they roam around in search of gurus or perfect masters. They create an image in their minds and visit gurus expecting them to live according to the image they have created. Soon they get disappointed because their fantasies are never materialized and never come true. Real masters also search for a good student. By the grace of God, when the master meets his disciple, they immediately know each other. The guru and disciple relationship is purely selfless, and there is no give and take in it. If there is any expectation and selfishness in this relationship, it is short-lived faith, based on emotionalism. In the path of the yogic tradition, the guru/disciple relationship is deeper than the father/son relationship. It is a divine relationship for the Divine alone and for nothing worldly.

Mantra Yoga

Mantra yoga is one of the branches of tantric yoga, a very effective way to awaken the fountainhead of knowledge. In this method, certain specific sounds are uttered and mentally remembered. In a general sense, these special formulas are composed of certain sounds or syllables that have special meanings and effects. There are three main ways of using the mantras: they are chanted loudly, they are uttered silently, and they are remembered mentally. The mantras that are remembered mentally generate powerful energy. The power of mantra is immense. Mantra means "that which liberates the mind from distractions." In the beginning, students do not understand the science of mantra. By constant and prolonged repetition with intense feeling and full concentration, mantra consciousness is strengthened. In this way, mantra siddhi is attained. Unless the mind is purified and well-trained, mere mantra recitation produces little solace and no effect. Mantra is endowed with the power of action and vibration, and as such it circulates through the whole body, energizing the vital (pranic) sheath, which is helpful to all the pranic vehicles. It generates a subtle energy like a flame of fire.

The imperceptible sound of the inhalation and exhalation is also considered to be a mantra. The sound that is heard by the mental ear is *hamsa, ham* being the outflow, and *sa* being the inward motion. This sound also is philosophically interpreted as *aham,* which means "this," and *sa,* which means "that"—this individual soul is essentially the universal Truth. When the awareness of this sound is strengthened, the student can remember it 21,600 times in twenty-four hours.

There are many *bija* mantras, which are used to understand the nature of different chakras. *Bija* means "seed." It signifies the kind of energy that illumines each chakra. Every chakra—or spiritual center—is aroused by certain bija mantras that bestow powers to the practitioner. When a sound is repeatedly created, the vibrations of the sound make a form, and that form is called a *devata*. The sound and the form remain inseparably one, like cause and effect. By creating the sound, the form appears.

The senses quickly respond to the vibration within certain limits, and if the limits are exceeded either way, the organs become insensible to these impulses or vibrations. Likewise, a stimulus to nervous matter effects a change in the matter by a reaction in it. When the repetition of the stimulus increases, the changes occur following a specific reaction. Until then, a constant repetition occurs in the nervous energy that is stimulated. Likewise, a voluntary change is brought about in the nervous system by breathing, along with the practice of the mantra. Mantric formulas are the most secret and esoteric of all yoga practices. There are very few mantras that are used with breath awareness. They are soft sounds like hamsa, soham, or Om. Other mantras create jerks and frequent pauses in the breath. Those who practice mantra with a deep inhalation and exhalation will realize that the flow of the breath is obstructed by the mantras which are not supposed to be used with inhalation and exhalation.

The yogi, focusing his attention on the sound of the mantra, practicing faithfully and regularly, attains mantra siddhi, in which mantra flows uninterruptedly and effortlessly. Technical repetition of mantra engages mind but does not yield much benefit. But when mantra is remembered with feeling and meaning, all the vibrations created by the mantra sound make the mind joyous and prevent it from distractions and dissipation.

Awakening Kundalini According to Tantra Yoga

Tantra yoga is the most misunderstood and abused of all practices. These sacred systematic and advanced practices for leading the aspirant to the highest state of consciousness have been caricatured in the West in a crude and superficial way. Tantra philosophy is the highest among all the practical philosophies of the East. In tantra yoga, the chakras are used as centers of worship of Shakti, the primal force and mother of the universe. Tantra literature is the richest of all spiritual literatures, but a fortunate few have the opportunity to meet the right guide. In reality, the subject matter of kundalini awakening is discussed in detail in tantra literature. In tantric literature, the awakening of this force is systematized and organized, and with the help of a competent teacher, any aspirant can awaken the kundalini and lead it to its final abode of Shiva, the union of the individual soul and the cosmic soul.

According to tantric philosophy, this universe is a manifestation of pure consciousness. In the process of manifestation, consciousness divides itself into two aspects, neither of which can exist without the other. One aspect retains a static quality and remains identified with unmanifested consciousness. In tantra yoga this quality is called Shiva and is conceptualized as masculine. Shiva is depicted as being absorbed in the deepest state of meditation—a state of formless being, consciousness, and bliss. It remains aloof in manifesting the universe. Shiva has all the power to be, but no power to become; he has no power of manifestation. Consciousness, as the power that manifests the whole world, arises out of this source as being. The other part of this polarity is a dynamic, energetic, and creative aspect that is called Shakti. Shakti is the great Mother of the universe, for it is from her that all forms and names are born. Shakti is the subtlemost power of the universe. She manifests herself as matter, energy, mind, and life force.

These two principles are inseparably united, but in the manifested world, an illusion of separation is created between pure consciousness and its manifestation. Shakti is a projection of consciousness that veils the pure consciousness from which she was projected. The innumerable illusory manifestations, termed *maya,* bring forth that which is called the universe. After eons of time when the universe is dissolved, it is drawn into the Shakti, to the same source that is the basis of its creation. Energy exists in two forms: dynamic and latent. All activities or forces of motion have a static background, and when consciousness manifests itself as the creative or dynamic principle, it divides itself into these two aspects. According to Tantra philosophy and mythology, the dormant force that supports the universe is symbolized by a serpent-like, coiled-up energy.

According to this philosophy a human being is like a miniature universe—that which is found in the cosmos already exists within the microcosm. Every individual is governed by the same principles that govern the universe. The human storehouse has surplus energy that remains unused for maintaining human life. This energy is symbolized as a resting serpent at the root of the spinal column. This energy is the static support of the entire body and all its pranic energies; it is the divine force in the human body. The dynamic aspect of energy that provides the working force for the body evolved from that energy of Shakti and is called prana. As electrical energy is more subtle than mechanical energy, pranic energy is more subtle than electrical energy. This energy and the way it functions and the channels it uses for its functioning are thoroughly studied by yogic science. The flow of prana has an intricate network of channels called nadis, connecting the body and mind and keeping the entire organism in functional order. This is the vital force of Shakti, which is the organizing force around the chakras.

The Chakras

According to Tantric texts, it is very necessary for a student of this path to have a clear and comprehensive knowledge of the chakras before he starts practicing the process of awakening kundalini. Yoga science is very complex and extensive. It includes the science of the body and knowledge of the nervous system and other energy levels that govern bodily functions. In addition, careful study of the mind, its modifications, and all states of consciousness, as well as the philosophy of the universe and human relationships, are included. Tantra philosophy integrates all these various levels of knowledge and energy. All the diverse areas of science, psychology, and philosophy are integrated, and all facets of oneself are coordinated by means of sincere efforts. By bringing them together within the field of inner life for learning to explore the inner world, thoughts, and emotions, the student attempts to unveil all the mysteries of the various levels of life and experiments with experiencing different aspects of his being and different reactions of the world.

The framework provided by the chakras, or center of consciousness, provides this facility. The student of Tantra studies these centers, their nature, and their interrelationships. The more he understands the various psychological and philosophical concepts, the more he finds it necessary to know all the bodies within the framework of the physical body, which operate on levels different from it but yet are coordinated with it.

The first of these is the pranic body, and more subtle is the mental body. After carefully examining the entire human being in its totality, we find that matter, energy, and mind alone do not complete the human existence. Underneath lies a basic principle, that which we call pure Consciousness. Consciousness is most often compared to a light, and the different bodies are like lampshades that cover it. These shades are made of different material, color, and qualities. Each shade reflects light to a certain degree and modifies it according to its properties. The outermost shade is the densest one, and the light that it sheds is always dim. If we remove each of them, the light becomes brighter. Because of the way these bodies conceal the light of consciousness, they are termed sheaths, or coverings. These bodies, or sheaths, do not function independently; they have a meaningful relationship because they are connected and coordinated. These connections are maintained by the chakras, of which there are mainly seven.

Manifestation of the cosmic force is expressed through these centers, which energize and govern corresponding regions of the body. Kundalini is manifested in the form of each center. The result is a particular frame of reference through which the individual experiences the world. For example, when mind and energy are expressed through anahata chakra, one becomes loving and is able to control emotional energy. Similarly, when mind and energy are predominantly expressed through swadisthana chakra, one is preoccupied with thoughts of sexuality. Each center has its own corresponding plane of reality to which the mode of experience corresponds.

The first chakra, at the base of the spine, is called *muladhara,* the root support chakra. This center is related to the instinct for individual survival. Insecurity, fear, and paranoia are the major feelings associated with it. The terror of total annihilation disturbs people at this level and shades their view of the world. The element for this chakra is earth, the color is yellow, and the sense is smell. Colonic and bowel diseases are related to this center. Integration at the anal center gives a feeling of stability, security, and groundedness.

The second chakra is located above the genitals. It is called *swadhisthana,* which means "her own abode." This center is concerned with the survival of the species, and with issues of sensuality and sexuality. Individuals preoccupied at this level view the world from the perspective of pleasure gratification, particularly sexual pleasure, and feelings of lust or repression prevail. The poles at this level are masculinity and femininity, and integration yields a sense of androgyny and an appropriate, controlled expression of sexuality. Diseases of the urinary and reproductive systems are related to imbalances at this level. Water is the element for this chakra, the color is creamy white, and the sense is taste.

The third chakra is located at the solar plexus. It is called *manipura,* which means "filled with jewels." This center deals with competition and the survival of the ego. Issues of domination and submission, of aggression and passivity, are related to it. Integration at this level yields cooperation, assertiveness, and dynamic energy. This center deals with the assimilation of food, and digestive disorders indicate issues at this level. Fire is the element for this center, the color is red, and sight is the sense.

The heart center, located between the breasts, is the fourth chakra. It is called *anahata,* which means "unstruck sound." Anahata chakra divides the body into two hemispheres; the upper and the lower. The three centers below the diaphragm represent the primitive expression of consciousness and are concerned with the instinctual gross aspects of human beings. They are closely related to the physical and sensual world and desires to obtain pleasureful objects. These chakras have a tamasic influence on human life. Negative emotions are related to these centers, and dwelling at these levels indicates a lower level of human development. But when consciousness rises above the horizon of the diaphragm, one becomes truly human and the higher consciousness dawns. The anahata chakra motivates one to be active and rajasic, but at the same time, it is considered to be a center that gives emotional maturity and leads one to sattva. Anahata is related to the unconditional giving of love, to offering nurturance and service. Pure compassion, selfless love, sensitivity, and empathy are the attributes of this center. Just as the heart and lungs nourish the entire body and the mother's breasts nurture the baby, one who has attained this level nurtures others. There is no sense of separateness from others at this level. It is at this center that upward and downward moving forces meet, and the star of David and the cross symbolize its central function. Air is the element for this center, the color is light gray, and the sense is touch.

The fifth chakra is located at the hollow of the throat. It is called *visuddha* chakra, which means "purified." It is the seat of creativity and receptivity. The infant accepting nurturance from the mother exemplifies this center, and devotion, surrender, trust, willingness, and creativity are the qualities related to it. Musicians and artists are said to have their energy concentrated here. Integration at this level yields creativity and the ability to grow and evolve. The element for this center is air, the color is blue, and the sense is hearing.

The sixth chakra is located at the center between the eyebrows at the "third eye." It is called *ajna* chakra, which means "command." The qualities of introspection and discriminative intellect are related to this center. One who has attained this level has inner vision, sees all things clearly, and has higher intuitive knowledge and wisdom. He has attained sushumna by integrating the right and left polarities, ida and pingala, and thus he can tap both logical judgment and open intuition. The element for this center is mind, and the color is clear.

Visuddha and ajna, which correspond to the cervical and pituitary centers, represent spirituality and the desire to obtain the experiences of the inner world. These two centers help the student in understanding the internal states and the potential within. Creative intelligence, wisdom, and intuition are experienced from these two chakras, which are dominated by sattva, serenity, and tranquility. There are many subtle chakras above the ajna chakra, culminating in the seventh chakra, the center of pure consciousness, at the crown of the head. It is called the thousand-petaled lotus, *sahasrara.* This is the abode of Shiva, of pure Consciousness. One who has attained this level is in a state of samadhi. Here the individual self and the cosmic Self merge.

Ordinarily, the individual is polarized, with Shiva residing at the sahasrara and kundalini Shakti lying dormant at the base of the spine. Then only a fragment of energy of the kundalini is dynamic, and the vast reservoir of the Shakti remains dormant. Human beings remain ignorant because they are not aware of this vast reservoir and are not able to use it for the attainment of the purpose of life. Those who are capable of transforming it from its latent to its active stage become dynamic. If there is anyone dynamic in any avenue of life, it is because of the power of Shakti or kundalini. The transforming experience, though rare, is only possible after awakening the kundalini in a systematic manner, under the guidance of a teacher who knows the subject both practically and theoretically.

The experience of awakening kundalini leads to unusual experiences. This practice comprises not only awakening but also systematically watching her through each of the chakras to the abode of Shiva, sahasrara chakra. This union is the highest, according to Tantric literature. When the student is able to achieve this union, he becomes fully aware of all the dimensions of his life, and he is illumined. It is a process of evolution in which a human being comes to realize his essential nature and he abides in that state of pure Consciousness. The body and its functions are used as instruments. The scriptures say that the union of Shiva and Shakti generates a nectar that continues to sustain the body in this superconscious state.

Three Schools of Tantra Philosophy

There are three prominent schools that have different ways and methods of awakening the kundalini. These three main schools of Tantra are: *kaula, misra,* and *samaya.* The aim and object of these three schools is to lead the aspirant to be successful in the world and to attain the purpose of life. The highest state of union or enlightenment is accomplished. These three tantric schools explain different ways and methods of awakening this primal force and leading it to the abode of Shiva.

The Kaula School

According to Tantra philosophy, aspirants are divided into three categories, and each of these is the focus of one of the three schools of tantra. The first category is aspirants who are not very intellectual and have less awareness. For such a category of aspirants, the kaula school offers something concrete to practice involving that which can be touched, sensed, and felt in the external world. In this school Shiva and Shakti are represented by male and female. This school acknowledges that suppression and repression or sexual acts performed in ignorance can lead the aspirant to many serious psychosomatic diseases. Realizing this fact, this school teaches him the way of channeling the sexual energy for the attainment of spirituality. Those who do not know the subject misunderstand the concept of Shiva and Shakti principles, the worship, and the rituals performed.

In the kaula school of Tantra, external worship—*bahya*

yajna—is performed, and the male and female principles are used for uplifting body consciousness to divine consciousness. Western students think that Tantra means doing sex, but this is absolutely incorrect. In Tantra practices, the male and female principles relate with one another as embodiments of Shiva and Shakti, rather than merely being two individuals performing the sexual act.

The kaula school believes that the fountainhead of all motivations of human life arises from one source, and that is called *kama.* From kama arises emotions and thoughts. If this source is not properly understood and controlled, it dissipates all the energy channels and leads them only to the groove of sexual life. Sex is a powerful and primitive urge in every creature, and human history records that many crimes and murders have their root in this powerful motivation. The kaula school teaches one to analyze, understand, and spiritualize this urge first. This school believes that that which can be a constant source of distraction and dissipation of human resources can also be a means of liberation.

In this school brahmacharya is not at all ignored. *Brahma* means Shakti; *charya* means the way of directing it. This is the only school that has understood the sexual urge and uses it as a part of worship. Various religions and cultures do not like to discuss and understand this urge openly, but the kaula school has many scriptures on this subject. The rituals are not explained in those scriptures, however. *Prayoga Shastra* are different from the philosophical texts. Only a competent teacher can give a logical explanation of these practices. This school believes in practicing disciplines with mind, action, and speech. It does not believe in the use of sex freely and frequently, anywhere and everywhere for sense gratification. It is a worship, a ritual for attaining siddhi.

All the schools of Tantra believe in *bhutashuddhi,* a purification process that includes body, mind, and samskaras.

After this is accomplished, students are trained to perform the rituals for awakening kundalini, the serpent power that remains dormant. There are two methods of rituals usually practiced by the students of this school. One is a system called *panchamakara,* and the other is called *ashtamakara.* The second rare method of practicing the ritual is found only in the hills of Assam. In the kaula way of practicing rituals, five objects of worship are used. They are: *madya, mansa, mina, mudra,* and *maithuna*—wine, meat, fish, postures, and sex. Madya is wine which is prepared by forest herbs picked with definite rituals so that the mind is not dissipated and attends the ritual with full concentration. This wine is not like ordinary wines; the purpose is not getting drunk or losing consciousness. Mansa, or meat, is used in this ritual with the concept that the principle of "*jivo jivasya bhaksanam*"—one jiva is food of another jiva. The use of fish is equally important in the ritual. The cleanest meat one can find is fish, if it is obtained from a clear, clean river.

After careful study of body language, we find that the body moves toward certain directions when one expresses certain feelings. These gestures are mainly so unconscious that one normally does not notice them. The school of tantra clearly studies body language and the useful mudras, which are called seals. The body is prepared to be in a state of fitness so it can perform rituals. No discomfort is allowed, so that mudras can be properly applied and the ritual performed accurately. This school practiced certain postures long before the science of hatha yoga was systematized. Those mudras and postures that help the male and female—representatives of Shiva and Shakti—are performed, and specific mantras are uttered.

Maithuna is a natural and spontaneous urge in all creatures. The sexual act is spiritualized between the two principles as a union and not only as a mere sexual act. The pious ritual is performed by the two principles of Shiva and Shakti as a worship. This school believes that all the obstructing or stumbling qualities and objects can be converted as means for awakening the primal force, kundalini. Kaula practices are actually the training programs for having control over the lower desires of mind and the physical necessities of the human body. The sexual act is thus a ritual and the aspirant is strictly warned not to use this ritual for any sort of sense gratification. This school believes the union of the male and female principles gives joy, and if that joy is expanded, one can attain eternal joy. Ordinarily human beings do not know how to attain the eternal joy. Therefore this school teaches the aspirant to awaken the latent force and worship her at muladhara.

The Misra School

The teachings of this school are higher and deeper than those of the school of kaula. This school believes in external rituals and also, at the same time, meditation in anahata chakra. That is why it is called *misra*; misra means "combined" or "mixed," where two schools meet. This school has a vast bulk of literature and is practiced by many aspirants in various states of India, Tibet, and Southeast Asia. These schools strictly observe secrecy of their practices for fear of being abused by pleasure seekers. It teaches aspirants to perform their actions with nonattachment along with *upasana*—devotion. The combination of these two has given the name *misra* to this school. In the entire *agama* literature, the awakening of kundalini is the central theme. By meditation on this, or worshipping the universal mother in anahata chakra, the kundalini is awakened and led to the anahata chakra, which is the center of the upper and lower chakras of the human body. This method of worship is called *antaryaga,* "internal worship," or *manasa puja,* "mental worship." It is a ritual without objects, performed mentally at the center between the breasts, anahata chakra. In this way a direct and conscious relationship with the Shiva and Shakti principles is established within. The aspirant is able to unite these two principles, which are inseparably one.

This inner worship, or *antaryaga,* makes the mind inward and one-pointed. The kaula and misra schools perform external and internal rituals and believe in attaining certain powers, which are called siddhis. In the misra school, the kundalini is awakened and led to the anahata chakra and worshipped there. In this worship, *manas puja* is performed.

Both *bhukti* (material well-being) and *mukti* (liberation) are attained by those who master the misra practices. There is vast literature available in the *agamas,* which have many commentaries available for the student of this path.

The Samaya School

The highest of all schools is *samaya.* This school is purely yogic without any external rituals; it is very systematic and scientific. It is the purest and finest method of awakening kundalini. The word *samaya* means "I am with you." This is the highest of all the schools of Shakti worship because its philosophy and practice lead the aspirants to *moksha*—liberation. This school practices nonattachment to the external objects of pleasure. The accomplished yogis who follow this path carefully select their students and prepare them to awaken the kundalini and lead it, illuminating all the chakras to the abode of Shiva, which is in the crown of the head, sahasrara. In this path, upward traveling or channeling the energy is one of the prominent practices. Such an aspirant is taught not to waste the semen but to direct the secretion of the testes and glands by a particular method of generating heat and evaporating it upward. This is done through the tube called the centralis canalis. This initiation was common during the Vedic period but is rare today.

When the student is trained to complete preliminaries and when his meditative posture has become steady, then he is led to the higher level. Siddhasana, called the accomplished pose, is perfected, and the knowledge of bandhas and pranayama is imparted extensively. In this school, advanced mudras like khechari and *maha* mudra are practiced. The raja yoga system and the system of samaya are very close, but the samaya practices are more systematic and finer than the raja yoga practices. This path is practiced by a very few yogins. The samaya school is the most advanced school in all of yoga.

Bhutashuddhi seems to be important before one makes meditative effort to awaken kundalini. This is a purification process that uses mantra recitation coupled with pranayama practices. Through the bhutashuddhi *kriya,* or cleansing practice, the conscious and unconscious aspects of mind are completely purified. Ajna chakra is the focus point for meditators before they perform antaryaga, or internal worship, in the sahasrara. The student experiences unbelievable and inexplicable joy and the mind spontaneously goes beyond time, space, and causation. Such a state is acquired by the aspirants of this path, and they feel the presence of the union of Shiva and Shakti. This constant presence leads the student's mind to the abstract attributeless state of bhakti. The aspirant becomes like a divine child, enjoying the perennial presence and experiencing the eternal union of Shiva and Shakti. When Shiva and Shakti are united it is called a state of *Paramashiva.* A constant awareness of Shiva and Shakti is the goal of this school. The student is liberated by attaining this state.

Sri Vidya

Among all the spiritual traditions, the tantric tradition is the most ancient, and among all the schools of tantra, samaya is the highest. The school of samaya is profound, with its philosophy and practices; the samaya school practices Sri Vidya. All the vidyas explained in the Tantric texts originate from Sri Vidya, the mother of all vidyas. Sri Vidya is known to

बिन्दुत्रिकोणवसुकोणदशारयुग्ममन्वश्रनागदलसंयुतषोडशारम् ।
वृत्तत्रयं च धरणीसदनत्रयं च श्रीचक्रमेतदुदितं परदेवतायाः ॥

श्रीचक्रम्

students as the symbol of the law of manifestation. The process of manifestation emanates from the ultimate Reality and moves into expansion by dividing this original unity into two: Shiva and Shakti. These are the latent and active aspects of consciousness dwelling in eternal unity. These two are represented in Sanskrit with the first and last letters of the alphabet: "a" and "h," which, like alpha and omega, signify everything in between them also. Thus, all the energy and elements in the universe, from the most subtle to the most gross, are held potentially within this seed of two phonemes. This perfect stillness, called *Samvit,* manifests into thirty-six gradations of cosmic evolution; the entire world is a continuous unfoldment of what is already in Samvit, and it will all dissolve back into this origin again. The sound principle of this manifestation, which emerges from the two bindus, Shiva and Shakti, is called *nada.* This entire process of expansion and dissolution is displayed graphically in the Sri Yantra.

All forms manifest from unity into diversity and then return again to unity. This is the eternal law of the cycle of the universe that is reflected in all things. In the philosophy of Sri Vidya, these two movements are known as dissolution (*laya-krama*) and evolution (*srstikrama*), and they are depicted by the concentric squares and circles and the interlaced, inverted and upright triangles of the Sri Yantra, which has the bindu point Samvit in its center. This union of Shiva and Shakti is called Mother Divine.

The cosmos manifests on various degrees and grades from this point, and in his spiritual journey, the aspirant travels inward from the periphery of Sri Yantra to the center. The students of Sri Vidya understand both the way of universal unfoldment and the way of individual dissolution. They are no longer caught in the web of maya, and they constantly enjoy the divine play of this cosmic energy. Students of this path meditate intensely on the Sri Yantra, realize the existence of Mother Divine, and practice japa with an *aksamala,* a mala of phonemes instead of beads that is comprised of all the cosmic sounds. This mantra is the auditory representation of the visual pattern described in Sri Yantra.

Sri Yantra thus maps the path of eternal return to inner wholeness and perfection. It shows that the origin of life is perfect bliss, peace, happiness, and wisdom and that its final destination must be the same. The subtlemost supreme internal worship practiced in the samaya school is called *bhavana,* and it is explained in the *Bhavanopanisad.* This scripture explains that that which is found in the individual self exists in the universe, and so in order to analyze and understand the universe, one can study the individual self. One's own body, mind, and spirit are the Sri Yantra. When all symbols and rituals are internalized, then the human body itself resembles Sri Yantra, and the student becomes one with the ultimate truth.

Just as one is comprised of the qualities of his mother and his father, so the nine triangles of Sri Yantra—five inverted and four upright—display the qualities of Shakti and Shiva. The inward spiritual journey mapped by Sri Yantra describes progress through nine stages, depicted by its nine circuits. The central point of Sri Yantra is like an island whose immense base remains hidden in the ocean of bliss, peace, happiness, and wisdom. In the samaya, the physical appearance of life—the human body—is the center of consciousness coming to the surface. It comes from the ocean of bliss, remains surrounded by it, and will return to it. To those who are aware of this reality, suffering, ignorance, and obstacles are unreal.

The components of this island, which comprise the physical body, are symbolized by precious gems, showing that it is an important means for higher attainment if utilized properly. On this island of gems, there is said to a celestial garden of wish-yielding trees, which represent the mind and desires. When undisciplined, this becomes a thick forest of suffering that hides the ocean of bliss. On this island are six seasons that are compared to the six tastes, which are the properties of food. Thus one's diet affects one's emotional life just as the growth of trees is affected by the seasons. The tastes are therefore important in developing attractive thoughts and desires that beautify the garden of mind. Regulation of food is therefore the foundation of all other regulations.

In the samaya school of internal worship the body and the mind are stilled and the student realizes that Sri Yantra is internal. Thus the nine levels of Sri Yantra have been equated to the chakras of the subtle body. Moving inward from the periphery, there are three sets of three chakras depicted in the design: muladhara, swadisthana, and manipura; anahata, vishuddha, and ajna; and two guru chakras and sahasrara. The *Saundarya Lahari*, the *Wave of Bliss*, of Shankara poetically explains the methods of practice for Sri Vidya, including the siddhis that are attained at various stages. In the samaya school, various chakras are focused on for different purposes.

According to the samaya school, after a series of initiations, the aspirant learns to meditate in the sahasrara chakra. This school alone knows the meditation method in the crown chakra or thousand-petaled lotus. Other schools of Tantra do not practice this most advanced meditative method. It should be remembered that the samaya school of tantra is the highest of all schools, and Sri Vidya is the most profound way of attaining the ultimate Truth. The goal of Sri Vidya is to attain turiya, the fourth state, which is beyond waking, dreaming, and sleeping. There is another name for Mother Divine, who is the residing deity of this fourth state, and that is *Tripura Sandari*, the fountainhead of beauty, bliss, and wisdom.

There are numerous scriptures available on tantric literature of all schools, but a competent guru is the only guide. Without his help, the aspirant cannot go beyond and attain liberation. Actually any spiritual practice that leads to the awakening of kundalini is worth trying to know, but the aspirant who has decided to practice this path should first study Tantric scriptures and then prepare himself to take this voyage and not go in search of a guru but start working with himself. The first requisite is to have a healthy body—a disease-free body; second, a balanced or tranquil mind; third, an intense desire to attain the truth. In fact, in great traditions, most of the spiritual practices are clearly and systematically explained. Tantra literature is the highest of all, which deals with this subject in a very systematic manner. In all paths the aspirants may experience moments of ecstasy and illumination, but there is only one path that helps the student to experience such phenomena at his will.

The yogic practices are explained in tantric literature and practiced under the guidance of a teacher who has himself awakened this latent force and led it to the crown chakra. He is the awakened master and the representative of a perennial tradition. Such a master, through a series of initiations, guides the aspirants to their goal. The first initiation is the imparting of a mantra, a seed sound, and when this mantra is assimilated in the unconscious mind and becomes a part of the aspirant's life, then he is taught to practice the mantra in conjunction with a number of coordinated spiritual exercises and mental and physical disciplines to purify him for the next step. The next step of initiation is inner *antaryaga,* a special method of meditation that helps mind in looking within. This way, a series of gradual steps are introduced to him. One of the most difficult steps is *upward traveling,* and the highest of all is *shaktipata diksha,* in which the master directly transmits his energy, which enables the student to remove the final obstacles. The advanced student of this path sometimes unconsciously influences those around him in the same way that a magnet influences metal objects in its proximity. It should be understood clearly that a master or a siddha only influences those who are already on the path. In shaktipata diksha, the influence is experienced in a fully conscious and extremely intense way. Through a touch or a gaze, or even without any touch or gaze, a real master is able to transform the consciousness of his closest disciple into a blissful state. But no real master ever gives such an initiation to unprepared students. Shaktipata removes the last stumbling block of samskaras and thus hastens the process of awakening the latent force. This experience is not frequently repeated. When a master works with his student, it is not on the gross or physical level, and the master is not alone in dealing with this powerful force. He has behind him the long tradition of the sages, of which he is only a representative.

The search for truth is an eternal quest of human life. The search does not stop by performing karmas, doing one's actions skillfully, lovingly, and selflessly and then offering the fruits of actions as a worship, but a few great men renounce the worldly possessions so that they can devote their time and energy wholly for the attainment of enlightenment. Such renunciates are great and no doubt worthy of reverence. But in the philosophy of Tantra, the aspirant does not renounce the world or sacrifice any of the so-called pleasures of the world, which are usually considered to be obstacles on the path. In this path, no renunciation and no sacrifice is made, but conquest is the goal.

Artha, dharma, kama, and *moksha* are the main goals of human life. *Artha* means having sufficient means in the external world so that the bare necessities of life do not consume time and energy in concern for external success. But *dharma* means that all the means that we gather together should be earned through righteousness only. *Kama* means the prime source of all desire, which should be carefully understood and channeled for attaining the height of spirituality, the prime goal of life. *Moksha* means liberation from all bonds of samskaras and the ones we create in this lifetime. Such freedom is the goal of tantra philosophy and its practices.

Conclusion

Conclusion

For choosing a path a student should first examine whether he has a burning desire to attain the purpose of life and to follow and practice the path sincerely and faithfully. He should then study his abilities and the predominant qualities of his personality. There are three qualities of mind, called *sattva, rajas,* and *tamas,* and every human being has these qualities in certain degrees and grades. One should be honest in carefully examining one's own predominant motivating qualities before he chooses a path. The sattva quality motivates the whole being to know, analyze, and realize the purpose of life. With the help of this quality, an aspirant can follow and practice any path and is always successful.

A student should also learn to understand whether he is active, emotional, or intellectual. There are aspirants who like to lead an active life; their personalities are controlled by rajas. The path of karma yoga is recommended to active aspirants. In the path of karma yoga one surrenders the fruits of his actions to others. His duty is a worship for him. Thus he remains free from the bonds of self-created miseries and attains liberation. The path of bhakti yoga is recommended to those who are emotionally oriented. In this path, the aspirant channels his emotions positively, and through devotion and surrender becomes one with the divine. The path of jnana yoga is meant for those few who intellectualize everything. By contemplating on the prime questions of life, such an aspirant finally realizes the truth and attains that state of wisdom in which all questions are resolved.

Those who want to monitor their progress and whose minds are scientifically oriented are advised to follow the path of raja yoga, for it is very systematic. It is exactly as though someone is treading a path on which milestones indicate his progress. The path of laya yoga or kundalini yoga, which awakens the primal force, is a highly technical path for which the aspirant should prepare himself before he begins. Those who want to realize and attain their human potentials and tap the vast reservoir of energy within themselves, awaken the primal force and lead it systematically upward, experiencing all the levels of consciousness and finally realizing the center of consciousness. When one attains this state, he also realizes that the individual self and the cosmic Self are one and the same.

Awakening kundalini through hatha yoga practices can be dangerous for two reasons: without discipline, the body and pranic vehicles cannot be trained, and without an accomplished teacher, the aspirant does not receive guidance when it is needed. Practicing only with the help of books can be injurious to the aspirant's health and may result in permanent damage to the nervous system and brain. It is good to practice hatha yoga, and it is equally healthy to practice the basic exercises of pranayama for accomplishing physical fitness and mental health. But the advanced techniques of pranayama, mudras, and bandhas could, if not properly practiced and executed, be a source of incurable disorders. Many seekers begin practicing their spiritual discipline as an ego trip wanting to experience extraordinary powers in order to gain control over and exploit others. Such seeking pollutes the path of spirituality and confuses many innocent beginners.

The path of Tantra is meant for a very fortunate few, especially for those who have a profound knowledge of the various schools of philosophy and who are prepared to practice the tantric way of life in which the male and female represent the two cosmic principles called Shiva and Shakti. Some choose to follow the external way of worship and others choose the external and internal both. But rare are those who follow the path of samaya, the highest of all paths of yoga and Tantra. In this path, the aspirant does not desire any siddhi. This is a meditative order that does not believe in any sort of rituals of any type. In this path the primal force is worshipped as the Mother Divine. The kaula and mishra schools strive for success in the external world as well as liberation—bhukti and mukti. But according to samaya, sushumna awakening after *bhuta-shuddhi* (internal and external purification) seems to be the first requisite. Then kundalini is awakened, and in the third step it is led to sahasrara and not allowed to flow again to the lower levels of consciousness. The path of samaya is the highest of all, in which the accomplished teacher imparts the knowledge of Sri Vidya to the prepared student. Such an aspirant attains the fourth state, turiya, the highest goal of human life. It is a state beyond. No other school of philosophy and yoga explains and experiences the transition period between death and rebirth. When a student meditates on the sahasrara chakra, the thousand-petaled lotus in the crown of the head, he receives the knowledge of consciously casting off his body and goes through the transition period very consciously. He knows the mystery of life hereafter. Such yogis are rare.

For following and practicing any of the paths, the aspirant should learn to follow its disciplines with mind, action, and speech. A student should not worry and bother about finding proper guidance, for the quest for Truth itself always provides the necessary guidance. When a student is prepared and receptive he receives guidance through the teachings and sayings of the great spiritual sages, through his own conscience, through living teachers, or sometimes through prophetic dreams or meditation. When one is following the right method, one finds peace and remains joyous and calm. These signs and symptoms are clear indications of the progress of the aspirant. To be successful, one should first have a burning desire to tread the path. Then one should have full determination, and should constantly make dedicated effort and be regular in his practices. When one becomes aware of the reality, then he commits himself to follow the path. Those who are committed to the path will accomplish their goal. The paths differ but the goal is only one.

Om. Peace, peace, peace.

About the Author

BORN IN 1925 in northern India, Swami Rama was raised from early childhood by a great Bengali yogi and saint who lived in the foothills of the Himalayas. In his youth he practiced the various disciplines of yoga science and philosophy in the traditional monasteries of the Himalayas and studied with many spiritual adepts, including Mahatma Gandhi, Sri Aurobindo, and Rabindranath Tagore. He also traveled to Tibet to study with his grandmaster.

He received his higher education at Bangalore, Prayaga, Varanasi, and Oxford University, England. At the age of twenty-four he became Shankaracharya of Karvirpitham in South India, the highest spiritual position in India. During this term he had a tremendous impact on the spiritual customs of that time: he dispensed with useless formalities and rituals, made it possible for all segments of society to worship in the temples, and encouraged the instruction of women in meditation. He renounced the dignity and prestige of this high office in 1952 to return to the Himalayas to intensify his yogic practices.

After completing an intense meditative practice in the cave monasteries, he emerged with the determination to serve humanity, particularly to bring the teachings of the East to the West. With the encouragement of his master, Swami Rama began his task by studying Western philosophy and psychology. He worked as a medical consultant in London and assisted in parapsychological research in Moscow. He then returned to India, where he established an ashram in Rishikesh. He completed his degree in homeopathy at the medical college in Darbhanga in 1960. He came to the United States in 1969, bringing his knowledge and wisdom to the West. His teachings combine Eastern spirituality with modern Western therapies.

Swami Rama was a freethinker, guided by his direct experience and inner wisdom, and he encouraged his students to be guided in the same way. He often told them, "I am a messenger, delivering the wisdom of the Himalayan sages of my tradition. My job is to introduce you to the teacher within."

Swami Rama came to America upon the invitation of Dr. Elmer Green of the Menninger Foundation of Topeka, Kansas, as a consultant in a research project investigating the voluntary control of involuntary states. He participated in experiments that helped to revolutionize scientific thinking about the relationship between body and mind, amazing scientists by his demonstrating, under laboratory conditions, precise conscious control of autonomic physical responses and mental functioning, feats previously thought to be impossible.

Swami Rama founded the Himalayan International Institute of Yoga Science and Philosophy, the Himalayan Institute Hospital Trust in India, and many centers thoughout the world. He is the author of numerous books on health, meditation, and the yogic scriptures. Swami Rama left his body in November 1996.

Main building of the international headquarters,
Honesdale, Pa., USA

The Himalayan Institute

FOUNDED IN 1971 BY SWAMI RAMA, the Himalayan
Institute has been dedicated to helping people grow physically, mentally, and spiritually by combining the best knowledge
of both the East and the West. Institute programs emphasize
holistic health, yoga, and meditation, but the Institute is
much more than its programs.

Our international headquarters is located on a beautiful
400-acre campus in the rolling hills of the Pocono Mountains
of northeastern Pennsylvania. The atmosphere here is one to
foster growth, increased inner awareness, and calm. Our
grounds provide a wonderfully peaceful and healthy setting
for our seminars and extended programs. Students from
around the world join us here to attend programs in such
diverse areas as hatha yoga, meditation, stress reduction,
Ayurveda, nutrition, Eastern philosophy, psychology, and
other subjects. Whether the programs are for weekend meditation retreats, week-long seminars on spirituality, months-
long residential programs, or holistic health services, the

attempt here is to provide an environment of gentle inner progress. We invite you to join with us in the ongoing process of personal growth and development.

The Institute is a nonprofit organization. Your membership in the Institute helps to support its programs. Please call or write for information on becoming a member.

Institute Programs, Services, and Facilities

All Institute programs share an emphasis on conscious holistic living and personal self-development. You may enjoy any of a number of diverse programs, including:

- Special weekend or extended seminars to learn skills and techniques for increasing your ability to be healthy and enjoy life
- Meditation retreats and advanced meditation and philosophical instruction
- Vegetarian cooking and nutritional training
- Hatha yoga and exercise workshops
- Residential programs for self-development
- The Institute's Center for Health and Healing, which offers holistic health services and Ayurvedic Rejuvenation Programs.

The Institute publishes a *Quarterly Guide to Programs and Other Offerings,* which is free within the USA. To request a copy, or for further information, call 800-822-4547 or 717-253-5551, fax 717-253-9078, email bqinfo@himalayan-institute.org, or write the Himalayan Institute, RR 1 Box 400, Honesdale, PA 18431-9706 USA.

Visit our Web site at www.himalayaninstitute.org.

The main building of the hospital, outside Dehra Dun

The Himalayan Institute Charitable Hospital

A major aspect of the Institute's work around the world is its support of a comprehensive Medical City in the Garhwal region of the foothills of the Himalayas. A bold vision to bring medical services to millions of people (most of whom are poor) who have little or no healthcare in northern India began modestly in 1989 with an outpatient program in Uttar Pradesh.

Today that vision has grown to include a large state-of-the-art hospital located between Dehra Dun and Rishikesh; a Medical College and nursing school; a combined therapy program that joins the best of modern medicine with the time-tested wisdom of traditional methods of healthcare; a rural development program that has adopted more than 150 villages; and housing facililties for staff, students, and patients' families.

The project was conceived, designed, and led by Swami Rama, who was a native of this part of India. He always envisioned joining the best knowledge of the East and West. And that is what is occurring at this medical facility, 125 miles north of New Delhi.

Guided by the Himalayan Institute Hospital Trust, the hospital, medical city, and rural development program are considered models of healthcare for the whole of India and for medically underserved people worldwide.

Construction and expansion continues. The hospital is now one of the best-equipped in India, and attention is turning to building primary and secondary satellite health centers throughout the mountainous regions where travel is difficult, especially for those in need of immediate medical attention. Future plans include a college of dentistry, a college of pharmacy, and research facilities to study Ayurveda, homeopathy, and yoga therapies.

The Himalayan Institute Press

The Himalayan Institute Press has long been regarded as "The Resource for Holistic Living." We publish dozens of titles, as well as audio and video tapes, that offer practical methods for harmonious living and inner balance. Our approach addresses the whole person—body, mind, and spirit—integrating the latest scientific knowledge with ancient healing and self-development techniques.

As such, we offer a wide array of titles on physical and psychological health and well-being, spiritual growth through meditation and other yogic practices, and the means to stay inspired through reading sacred scriptures and ancient philosophical teachings.

Our sidelines include the Japa Kit for meditation practice, the original Neti™ Pot, the ideal tool for sinus and allergy sufferers, and the Breath Pillow™, a unique tool for learning health-supportive breathing—the diaphragmatic breath.

Subscriptions are available to a bimonthly magazine, *Yoga International*, which offers thought-provoking articles on all aspects of meditation and yoga.

For a free catalog call 800-822-4547 or 717-253-5551, email hibooks@himalayaninstitute.org, fax 717-251-7812, write the Himalayan Institute Press, RR 1 Box 405, Honesdale, PA 18431-9709, USA, or visit our web site at www.himalayaninstitute.org.